Hose Tower at the downtown central Station #1 after a long night of multiple house fires. (Photo courtesy of the author)

TWO DARK THIRTY

TRUE STORIES TO INSPIRE TEACHING AND LEARNING IN OUR LOCAL HEROES

Marc Hill

smoky coast

Smoky Coast Press

BLURBS

"Marc has an enjoyable written style and the professional experience to catch and keep your attention. You can feel his heartfelt passion in the emergency services."
— David Briggs, Division Chief of Training,
City of Wausau Fire Department

"Two Dark Thirty is a must-read for not just those already in the emergency services field, but for those who may be considering stepping into one of the many positions available to serve your community and make a positive difference."
—Steve Prziborowski, Deputy Chief (ret.)
Santa Clara County Fire Department,
Founder/Owner of www.code3firetraining.com

"Two Dark Thirty offers insight to raw emotions and experiences that you can't learn until you've experienced them. By getting this book into the hands of our future it will encourage them and support them at a time we need them most."

—K. Raduechel

"Marc's captivating stories engrain the most valuable parts for teachers and trainers. Educators everywhere will wish they had this sooner!"

— Paul Czarapata, Battalion Chief (ret.)
City of Wausau Fire Department

About Author

Marc Hill has spent over twenty years in public service. He has taught every grade from middle through high school and college-level students. In small rural and larger urban settings. Marc has also served as an assistant coach, head coach, union president, principal, training officer, preceptor, and mentor. He has been selected as teacher of the year three times by his students. Marc also served as a volunteer firefighter and EMT before becoming a full-time Fire Chief and now serves the people of Wausau Wisconsin as a firefighter and paramedic and as an adjunct instructor for Northcentral Technical College. Recently he has earned the department's merit of core values award. Marc's passion for learning and serving inspired him to become an author. Marc is happily married and has three beautiful daughters.

Also By

Please check out the companion workbook for Two Dark Thirty to help inspire your own teaching and learning!

This book is dedicated to the men and women, in emergency services, who made the ultimate sacrifice for our communities and the local heroes who continue to take the watch and ensure our safety.

Acknowledgments

I want to take the time to thank all my family for the warmth, kindness, and positive support they have given me all these years. Especially my wife and soulmate Sara, who is always there to prop me up and support me on my wayward journeys. My daughters Annika, Piper, and Cora who have had to deal with their exhausted father after coming home from work and all the nights spent writing. They all enlighten my spirit and give me more reason to push forward than they will ever realize.

I'd like to thank my editor Gwendolyn Bristol for all her hard work in helping me make this book worthy of publishing.

Finally, I would like to send a big thank you to all my friends, Chief Paul Czarapata, Kelly Raduechel, Chief Steve Prziborowski, my father Michael Hill, and father-in-law Steve Bennwitz who helped me with the manuscript edits and proofreading.

I could not have done this without all your help and support.

CONTENTS

TWO DARK THIRTY

TRUE STORIES TO INSPIRE TEACHING AND LEARNING IN OUR LOCAL HEROES

MARC HILL

PREFACE

I wrote this book to be a guide. Think of it as a resource. It is the culmination of my humble experiences, thoughts, beliefs, skills, and actions over the past twenty-plus years in public service. I have had great opportunities to serve as a teacher, coach, principal, firefighter, and paramedic. My goal with this book is to combine my life's events with the most important aspects of teaching. These thoughts could help any instructor, mentor, leader, officer, organization, department, or agency become better at educating and training their new employees or students.

I have had two extraordinary careers, and I have a unique set of skills. I have taught 6th grade to college adults and every grade in between. My teaching has led me from small country schools to large suburban high schools. Having also risen through the ranks of the fire service, from a volunteer firefighter to a career firefighter, and chief, my trials and tribulations shaped me. I had the experience of being laid off three times, and I went through state workers' reeducation programs. I have seen firsthand how fast education changes over time, from using overheads and scantrons to online platforms and using mobile web-based applications. I understand how difficult it is to train, motivate, and get your students and crew to develop into the best versions of themselves.

This book is how I found success in both the fire-rescue service and in education, as well as what I have failed in and learned from over the past twenty years in public service. I hope you can take away a bit from my stories and thoughts to help you succeed on your path.

Introduction

My personality has always leaned toward explaining concepts and ideas to people. Even from the earliest age, I would try to explain how things worked, or at least how "I" thought they worked. I tend to always insert myself into situations where teaching is involved. Through all my education and experience, no one ever taught me "how" to be a successful teacher. Many classes explained what teaching was not really how to perform. I learned that lesson by doing, observing, and trying on my own, both successfully and in epic failure.

I am the eldest of three children. I was obligated to take care of my two younger sisters and make sure they didn't get into trouble. This taught me early on to be responsible and to look out for those who couldn't. My family moved around a lot when I was young. I attended four different elementary schools in three different states in a matter of two years. Although a bit destructive for a young boy developing, this forced me to learn how to make friends, be social, deal with change, and communicate. As I got older, I became more involved with sports in school, creating new requirements of time management, integrity, drive, toughness, determination, and teamwork.

We now know those earliest years are the most formative for children. They are the years when you find out a little about who you are and what you think is important. Those ideas may change as we get older. We get married and have children of our own. We move out of our parents' house and make a home for ourselves. We buy our first car and get our first jobs. In all those situations, we are challenged, but we adapt and achieve. We learn and we grow.

Though rarely acknowledged, part of being a successful teacher is learning from our mistakes and failures. Impart the life lessons you have mastered to your students. True education is the explanation of how to learn, comprehend, adapt, and apply our knowledge. It creates pathways for applying new understanding to new situations.

As you begin this book, remember, learning never stops. It is a marathon to the grave.

I wrote this book because I saw a need to address these topics and ideas. I've often noticed that many who find themselves in teaching positions are not familiar with basic educational topics. Within my own department, we have one, two, and three-year people training, with the experience of being the preceptors for our new probationary members. There was a lack of experience for this level of expectation. This book is designed for those individuals who find themselves in that precarious position. These lessons are from my own experiences, from the education I have earned, and the lessons I've independently sought out in life.

I fell into teaching when I was getting my bachelor's degree and found my skills lent well to it. Education is a simple concept, but

xxii   TWO DARK THIRTY

teaching is a real challenge. Many try, and few truly succeed. That is why there are so many books, speakers, videos, lectures, movies, and so on about those topics. What might work for one person might not work for another. To discover what you like or what works for you, you need to experiment, and you need to be okay with failing. To truly gain wisdom, a person needs to both succeed and fail.

Hence this book. This is my take on how I found success teaching and leading in the classroom and emergency services.

Being a teacher is one of the most important careers anyone can have. It is difficult to achieve anything without having learned it, observed it, or modeled it from someone else. As they say, teaching is the only profession that teaches all others. Teachers are all around us, and they are in the most unique places. Some people are teachers by profession, and others are teachers by chance and circumstance. In the end, a teacher is the distributor of knowledge. I will use the terms 'teacher' and 'instructor' interchangeably throughout the book.

When I talk about emergency services, I'm referring to fire, emergency medical services (EMS), and law enforcement. In emergency services, any outstanding teacher is also a leader, and any good leader is also a teacher. Within both fields and both positions, you must be able to do both. A great classroom teacher must set an example for their students and must show and emulate the behavior and actions they want to see in their students.

A teacher must be knowledgeable about their subject, much like a leader. The leader must be knowledgeable about the topics and about the potential issues that will arise from a situation. Leaders must be able to change and find a path to success. A teacher must have exceptional communication skills, know how to listen to their students, and be able to communicate the lessons in many ways, much like a leader must be able to communicate their mission and goals. A leader must be disciplined and humble, and so should a good teacher; both need to understand and have empathy with those they are trying to teach.

Teachers and leaders must have genuine integrity. They both need to have the ability, knowledge, and moral aptitude to know what is right and what is wrong. They must motivate themselves to achieve their objectives in the most ethical and moral manner possible. A good teacher should be approachable and someone you want to succeed for; a great leader motivates you to do your best because you admire them.

Being a great leader and being a great teacher are connected. They are not opposites, but they are both positions a person needs to be familiar with. Understand the importance of each, and remember, some learning is observed, not directly taught. Being successful in either does not mean being perfect. It's called the practice of teaching and the practice of leading because that is what you need to do: practice, over and over, always striving to make yourself better.

To get better every day, you need to know what to work on. Become familiar with your strengths and weaknesses. History shows us great teachers and leaders work every day to better themselves and improve their craft, constantly wanting to achieve greater things.

To know if you are right for a position, whether teaching or leading, you need to ask yourself if it is something you want to do for the best of others. No one goes into teaching to make big bucks and retire early to the beach. You become a teacher because you are enthusiastic about the subject and want to help anyone who wishes to learn more about it. You put others first.

The best times I had as a teacher were when I saw the eyes of my students light up. It's the point where the light bulb goes on, and they understand; they grasp it. You can see the understanding. You can see the comprehension in their eyes and on their faces. The achievement is there for all to see, and it's a wonderful feeling to know you had a part in creating that. You helped create the spark of learning in them that will light a flame of knowledge. It is miraculous.

I also experienced this spark when I coached athletics. I coached football, track and field, and weightlifting for many years in middle school, high school, and college. When you strive to help teach athletes a particular move or to show them the fundamentals of how to play a sport, you notice the same sort of light you see in their eyes when they have accomplished something new. Their entire demeanor changes and they portray confidence.

The same thing goes when you are in emergency services, when you have been given the responsibility to oversee a crew. Your organization has given you a mission goal or task to achieve. It is up to you to disseminate the information, come up with the tactics, and plan to bring your team successfully to the finish line. There are few experiences in life that will give you the satisfaction teaching can. Take the time to enjoy the ride.

The stories I share in this book are all ones that happened to me. The names were changed to protect the innocent. However, the essence of the story remains true. It is what I remember, and it is what I have learned from my experience. Let's start this journey to inspire teaching and learning in our local heroes.

Buckle up, here we go…

Fire Prevention Talks 2017. Firefighter Nick Gehring speaking to a group of 1st Grade students at our local Elementary School on the strangeness of firefighting gear. (Photo courtesy of the author)

Chapter One

WHERE DO I BEGIN?

"Tell me the facts and I'll learn. Tell me the truth and I'll believe. But tell me a story and it will live in my heart forever."
—*Native American Proverb*

It was the early morning, just past 2:30 AM, and the full moon was bright in the sky, casting a near-daylight shadow on the road. My partner and I were driving our ambulance back to the fire station from the hospital's emergency room (ER). To say we were exhausted would be an understatement. We had just finished our twelfth call that day and were on a stretch of back-to-back EMS calls in the past three hours. Our reports were stacked up and the paperwork was beginning to get mixed together in the center console of the ambulance. We left our comfortable beds at the downtown fire station just after 10 PM, having only been in them for twenty minutes, just long enough to warm the bed up. I was trying to finish my latest patient care report on the laptop when we got dispatched by our 911 call center for a patient lifting assistance and welfare check. Our local police department was also on its way to the scene.

The address was familiar, and so was the patient. Let's just say we were on a first-name basis. The gentleman was in his mid-twenties and had a dangerous alcohol and drug problem. He would often fall out of bed in his inebriated state and scream for help. Eventually, someone in his apartment building would grow tired of his screams and they would call 911.

We arrived on the scene and made our way into his apartment. As we walked down the dimly lit hallway, with all of our EMS gear, we noticed the apartment door was already open. Our police officers were already on the scene. We could hear muffled talking. As we slowly walked into his residence, our boots stuck to the linoleum floor as we walked through the kitchen. There were various states of half-eaten food, spilled liquids, garbage, and empty beer cans and bottles everywhere. As we rounded the corner, we found our patient lying on the floor next to his bed. However, this time was very different.

In prior visits, he usually had a pet boa constrictor snake next to his bed in a six-foot glass enclosure. We could see this time, when he fell, he must have tried to grab onto the aquarium and knocked it to the floor, breaking the glass and freeing the snake. Not only were we attending to a vodka-soaked patient covered in urine, feces, and broken, bloody glass, but now we were on the lookout for an escaped four-foot reptile that was slithering somewhere in the run-down apartment.

This, my friends, is what I refer to in our field as 'Two Dark Thirty.' My partner and I turned to each other with a shared look on our faces that said, "What else could go wrong?"

So, you may now be asking, why did I title the book 'Two Dark Thirty'? Isn't this a book about teaching? Many of the emergency services are also paramilitary in nature. They adhere to general rules of conduct and codes that are similar to military values and norms. Some of this comes as time-telling, such as using the 24-hour scale. Zero would mean midnight. It has been my experience many of our worst calls for emergencies happen at the witching hour, the time of night just after bars close. The time tends to be 02:30 AM, or in the term, I like to use, 'Two Dark Thirty.'

This is the time when emergency calls come in and wake up those who serve on the front lines of our communities. It's the middle of the night when you get a dispatch for a multiple-vehicle collision and rollover with entrapment of victims and both cars are on fire. Or there's a house fire, and someone is currently hanging out of the third-story window screaming for help. It's a 911 call from an apartment building where a savage fight has occurred; two people have multiple stab wounds, and blood is all over. Stress ramps up within seconds after you are woken up from a dead sleep by hearing the tones go off. This is when seconds count and all hell breaks loose.

At Two Dark Thirty, everyone in emergency services needs to be ready for those instances that occur at the least expected moment. When it comes to teaching and learning in emergency services, isn't it at these moments we can truly gauge our success... or shortcomings?

Acknowledging this up front helps set the tone for the seriousness that underlies the preparation, effort, and dedication we need to put forth, to be tremendously successful and to educate ourselves and others in this profession.

As an educator, you cannot ignore the heightened element of stress and still expect your students to lead and be ready for those instances that always occur in the middle of the darkest night. This book is designed to provide answers to those types of questions. I wrote it to support all in education—to become better and achieve more from my own thoughts, beliefs, and experiences—and in the end, to prepare our students to perform and excel at Two Dark Thirty.

Be a Storyteller

"The purpose of a storyteller is not to tell you how to think, but to give you questions to think upon."

—*Brandon Sanderson*

Gripping stories tell a tale. If you have ever read a great book, the author captivates you and brings you into the world you are reading. They immerse you in descriptions, characters, and plots. The same feeling happens when you listen to a story being told. If you tell stories in your class, you can grab the attention of your students. Once you have their attention, you can take them on a journey anywhere.

Stories and word-of-mouth teachings are the truest forms of communication and the first steps in education. Being a storyteller is paramount for any teacher. It is a skill that you must hone and develop. But don't think the stories have to be all about you. I tell tales all the time about my own experiences, but I also tell stories of what has happened to others.

Humans have existed on this planet for hundreds of thousands of years. The majority of the population has only been truly literate for the past 100–200 years. By literate, I mean being able to read and write.

For most of human history, only the extremely rich, kings and queens of nobility, and those who were members of protected classes, such as the clergy, could read and write. The powerful saw being literate as a way to control the population. Obviously, this all changed with the invention of the printing press. The powerful could no longer keep the information from spreading through the populace. Being literate spread education in the world and people started to ask questions, which led to change and advancement.

Before we could read and write, we learned by listening to and speaking about our history through stories. Humans have learned through word of mouth, or oral narratives, since the very beginning. The oral traditions of native peoples and those of our ancient ancestors all tell a story. They focused on life lessons and on passing knowledge of the local area. They were the hints, tricks, and life hacks to surviving in the world of that time.

I still believe it is a brilliant way to educate people and communicate information. Stories fascinate students and pull them into the lesson.

In ancient Greek times, the philosophers of Plato and Aristotle questioned everything and created stories to challenge thought. These short stories were meant to illustrate a moral lesson and give examples to their students, to make them think about their current beliefs. Jesus taught his biblical messages through stories and parables. Modern-day storytellers, such as authors, radio, and television and film directors, use the many forms of multimedia to captivate their audiences and bring them into a wondrous world of imagination. They set a stage to pull you into a new realm of creativity and put forth thoughts that can lead to investigation and learning.

Oral traditions have an obvious basis in the spoken and heard senses. We use our ears to hear and our minds and hearts to process those thoughts and feelings. Those senses are built into us. How many of us remember song lyrics and remember events based on when a song is played? Singing songs was an easy way to recite and memorize prayers and stories. We use that sense of hearing and relate it to what we see and are doing at that time. We are tied to remembering things based on our senses. Oral storytelling uses the sense of hearing and our brain's imagination to envision what we are hearing.

Storytelling is one of the most important ways to expand the knowledge of your students. They will remember your story about a topic or about why something happened far more than the specifics of the third chapter's fourth paragraph second line. To be a good teacher, you need to entertain. Be a storyteller. Engage your students in this thoughtful activity. Have imagination and be creative in your delivery.

Some characteristics of a good story are:

1. *Catching the listener's ear: the story is interesting and exciting.*

2. *Short and sweet: the story is the right length to explain but short enough to keep attention.*

3. *It has elements of drama or intrigue that make your listeners think and pay attention.*

4. *It draws a conclusion or has a moral lesson to it.*

5. *It is easy to understand and can be retold by the listener.*

I occasionally run into former students of mine from decades past who still refer to me as Mr. Hill or Coach Hill. I even work with two of my former students in my current fire department. One of my former students is now my supervising lieutenant. When I started in the department, it took him years to be comfortable enough to call me by my last or first name. Every time he saw me in the hallway or in the station, he would refer to me as Mister or Coach Hill. Everyone laughed and thought it was funny. It is and was.

Think of the last time you ran into a former teacher or coach of yours. Did you think you would call them by their first name? Usually not. To this day, I have a hard time swearing in front of my parents; I still think I will get in trouble.

When I see my former students, what they remember most about me as a teacher is my stories. I would take the time, in my prepping, researching, and reading, to find interesting tales to tell. Who doesn't love a good gossip tale about a double-cross or political intrigue? *Law and Order* has been on television for over twenty years, and there is a reason why it is so successful. There must be something to it, right? Each subject and lesson I taught had a story, much like this book has stories tied throughout each chapter. Stories captivate, and stories illustrate in our mind's eye the subject and help our brain to create memories and remember more information. This is essential for emergency service heroes, who must know the information by heart to act quickly and decisively in catastrophic conditions.

If you are enthusiastic about the subject and thoughtful, exciting, and entertaining in your delivery, you won't have trouble in your classes with discipline, grades, or comprehension. Those factors will all be taken care of naturally. This will be true because your students will see, feel, and hear your passion and excitement about the subject. Something as simple as telling a story illustrates your point and creates a better understanding for the student. It goes miles further than just writing notes and reading a PowerPoint presentation.

In my years of teaching experience, I have found bad teachers blame and make excuses. It's the bad teacher that says the students just don't get it because they aren't smart enough. It's a bad teacher that blames the parents or blames the district for lack of money or whatnot. They make excuses because they believe it is not their fault the students are failing. The hard truth is it is them. It has nothing to do with money, or technology, or anything tangible. Those are all excuses, and we need to look at ourselves first. What did we do or not do? Think about your lesson and think about how a story can add to it. Own what you teach in your lesson.

Students in ancient Greece did not have walls, roofs, or electricity, but they learned, grew, and developed the systems and features that enabled Western Civilization to become what it is today. Why? Because they told stories and used thought experiments. They discussed and challenged each other, and they pushed each other further.

A good teacher finds ways to reach their students no matter what the problem is. Take the time to realize what went right and what went wrong with your prior lesson. Reevaluate yourself. Did you use too much jargon or specific words no one understood? Did you talk over your audience and assume they had more experience than you had?

I'll talk more about evaluating later in the book. For now, consider being a storyteller to engage and entertain your students for positive results. It is not complicated. Remember to keep it simple, be clear in your expectations, and be honest with your students. Start by telling a story.

Engage Your Students

What was the most boring class you ever had in school? We all have had one or two, and some of us have had years' worth of boredom in school.

When I was in college for my bachelor's degree, I had a course called *History of the Copper Country*. As a social studies student it was a required course, but it sounded interesting to me. However, the professor who taught the course was far from it. He would come into the class and sit at a table in the front. Then for the next hour he would literally read from a binder of class notes. He would not get up, he would not look up, and he would not engage in discussion. There was no time to ask questions. He would come in at the exact time class stated and then start to read after taking attendance. He read right up to when class was scheduled to end. Needless to say it was a tough class to go to.

How many have had similar experiences? Many of those subjects were boring not because of the subject, but because of the teacher. If the teacher doesn't do a good job of relaying the information and keeping attention, students zone out. Do not be that type of teacher! Be active, passionate, and collaborative. You cannot be boring or monotone and expect to keep your students' attention.

Move and keep the attention shifting, by simply walking around the room. You can go from place to place within the room to change the direction of your voice, and you can keep people on task by coming closer to them. If you are teaching your class online via video, then raise and lower your voice. Keep changing your position on the screen and use your hands. Doing this will help to create attention for your students and will keep their focus.

Talk to your students. Ask questions. Sometimes, asking how the students want to learn is the best course of action. Engage them in the learning process. Lead them to the answers and guide them through the lesson material. Be appealing and captivating in your plans for your students. Talk to your students about the entire educational plan for the course.

Engaging a student can have many characteristics and can happen in several ways. As an example, you can start class with a funny video or cartoon to get the mood right. You could start by coming in dressed up in an interesting costume—or just start by telling a story. Bring the students into the lesson and have them participate. Be creative. Engage their minds, engage their learning spirits, and engage their thoughts and beliefs.

Define Your Expectations

An important task to remember is to clearly communicate your expectations. We have all been in lectures and in training where there are pockets of people gossiping and not paying attention. It's distracting when someone keeps getting up for coffee or to go to the bathroom, or when someone is texting on their phone during class. You need to be an example and model the behavior you expect.

You are the instructor; explain openly what you are doing and why, how, and when. Tell your students to straighten up, pay attention, and silence their phones for the next hour. Explain where the bathroom is if they don't know and tell them there is no need to get up because there will be ten-minute breaks every forty to fifty minutes.

You must set the tone. You are the teacher-leader in the class. Students need to know what you expect. Adults can be just like children. They enjoy order and routine. However, to follow the rules, they need to know what they are.

Never expect people to know how to act. That is an assumption. I can't tell you how many times I've had adult students act in a certain way when I assumed they should know better. The adage 'It's not the age but the maturity' is very true. In teaching refresher courses for emergency medical services (EMS) and firefighting, I have had students in their sixties and even their seventies acting and behaving like 3rd graders. I'm amazed when I must pull them aside and explain how their behavior is disrupting the group.

Because of my willingness to do the hard and uncomfortable communication, I never really had issues in the classroom with my management and discipline. Being a public-school teacher in middle and high school isn't much different from teaching adults in college. You will know when you need to be louder or move around. You will feel and observe it in the room. Those are some of the basics when it comes to classroom management and control.

You need to be a presence in the room. If you sit in the front, behind a desk, and you never get up or move around, people will nearly always choose to do something else. This is especially true when the topic to be covered is on the challenging side. Be engaging with your students and capture their attention but have clear expectations and be the example.

You Are No Imposter

Sometimes I have doubts about myself and my abilities. The fear of the unknown is natural. This usually occurs on the first day or in the days leading up to starting a new position or task. We all get butterflies in our stomachs. This is normal and usually goes away after you get settled into the position. But sometimes it does not go away, and the dreadful feelings stay with you and sometimes get worse. This continual feeling is a condition, and it has a name. It is called Imposter Syndrome.

People who suffer from this state have such massive doubt and trouble with the position they hold because they think they do not deserve it. They believe everyone is looking at them and will find out they are a fraud and they do not belong in the position they hold. They are waiting for the proverbial rug to be pulled out from under them and the giant spotlight to be cast on their failure. These individuals often feel there is no amount of training or increasing education they can do that will ever prepare them for this position. They have absolutely no faith or belief in themselves.

According to an article in *Psychology Today (1),* around 25–30% of high achievers may suffer from Imposter Syndrome. At least 70% of adults may experience impostorism at least once in their lifetime. It is important to note the article focused on high achievers. High achievers are the ones that have such grand expectations for themselves they develop this syndrome because of not being able to live up to their own expectations. Within the emergency services, we find a great many high achievers. The 'A-type' personalities dominate the firehouse. High achievers are great at having a solid drive. What is not known is how much self-doubt they have internally. They are great at portraying the right persona but inside they are crying. Impostorism becomes a problem when you let that doubt manifest and become a constant nagging thought in your mind. Start by knowing that we all begin at zero. We all start at a point where we must learn new ideas and new concepts.

We all occasionally have the feeling we are in over our heads. Do not let the feeling morph into something more serious, like Imposter Syndrome. You will be new at first and fresh out of the box, as we say sometimes. You will be the greenhorn, the new person. As time goes on and as you become more familiar with the job and the role that you play, you will become more comfortable with the position. This enables you to prepare students more effectively for Two Dark Thirty.

Yes, you can do it! Believe in yourself. If you have questions, ask. Find resources and others to help you. You are not alone. Feel free to go to the book website (twodarkthirty.com) and contact me there or post on the discussion board. We need to stick together. Have faith in yourself. You are not alone.

Attitude is Everything

"Weakness of attitude becomes weakness of character."
—*Albert Einstein*

Not every day can be perfect. We are human, after all, and our moods can change like the seasons or the weather. That being said, a good-quality teacher has an overall positive attitude and aura that is evident within seconds of meeting them.

You can tell how a teacher feels just by watching him or her walk into a room. Do they look confident and enthusiastic about the day's lesson, or are they staring at the ground and shuffling around the room? In our time as students, I think we can all agree and remember seeing this type of behavior in our instructors. You can feel the positive or negative presence. A positive attitude will be emitted as an aura of kindness, appreciation, knowledge, and genuine care. The best teachers want to see you do well and learn.

As a first-time teacher, walking into a classroom can be very intimidating. Everyone gets nervous. Remember to relax. Everything will be fine. Students can sense fear, so make sure you walk in with confidence. No one expects you to know everything, and if anyone tells you otherwise, they are liars or do not know what they are talking about. Take a breath. If this frightens you, accept it and use it to motivate yourself to be better. Your emergency services students will respect and respond to your courage, because they understand the need to act confidently when they're under stress, too.

If being in front of groups scares you, practice by putting yourself into situations where you are in front of people or groups. Sometimes the best way to learn is by throwing yourself right into it. Get out there and make yourself uncomfortable. Grow and learn from the experience. Find a Toastmasters club or other organizations to develop public speaking skills. Ask around if anyone needs help with a group presentation. Find what works for you and use it to make yourself better.

When you come in ready and full of a positive attitude, the students will pick up on this. They will see your confidence, and this will develop their trust in you as the instructor.

When I was teaching at a rural country middle school, my wife and I had our first daughter, and I went on paternity leave. During that time, I had a long-term substitute teacher, Ms. Smith, who was very smart and knowledgeable about the subjects I taught. She was eager and happy to find her first teaching position. I left her with detailed daily instructions and everything she needed to keep the ship running, just as I had done. It was simple, and I thought it foolproof.

However, within a week, Ms. Smith had major discipline issues and lost the student's attention and control. She was unsure of what to do and called me at home. She told me she followed my plans, but the students were not behaving, and everything was a mess. I could hear the upset and frustration in her voice. I told her to change things to suit her style of teaching; she did not have to be just like me. If the subject was covered, she could do whatever she felt she needed to do. Ms. Smith tried, and she attempted many strategies for the remaining time.

After six weeks, my leave ended, and I came back. The students were relieved to see me, and so was she. After Ms. Smith left, I asked the students why they misbehaved and what was so wrong. They said, in frank terms, they thought she didn't like them as students, and they didn't think she knew anything about the subjects. Being new, Ms. Smith went in with no confidence in herself and her abilities. The students immediately picked that up. She failed before she even started. Like sharks, the students smelled blood in the water. Ms. Smith was finished before she even began.

Attitude and confidence in yourself can go a long way. If you have doubts, and we all do, find something to be confident in. Practice the craft before you get there. Set yourself up for success. For many new teachers, having a prepared lesson will instill confidence. Believe in yourself and come in with a positive attitude.

Find Significance in What You Are Teaching

"Success is fine, but success is fleeting. Significance is lasting."
—Beth Brooke

Part of having the right attitude, confidence, and belief is understanding what you are teaching. Make sure you teach something you enjoy and find interesting. At the very least, find something interesting to you in the subject matter and spend time on that. Faking it will not work. We can all tell in the first few minutes of listening to someone's discourse whether they believe what they are saying.

Are you saying it with feeling? Are you motivated to teach this subject, or are you being told to get out there and tell students about it? When someone is speaking, if they do not know the material and do not want to be there, students can feel it. They shut off any kind of attention to the instructor and cease learning.

Do yourself a favor. If you don't find the subject interesting or are not excited about it in any way, shape, or form, then find someone who is. Bring in a guest speaker who cares to teach and talk about the subject. I guarantee if you ask around, you will find someone who has an interest and knowledge of the subject. It is okay to split the subject into parts and find guest teachers or lecturers to talk about the parts they love. Yes, you are becoming more of an event organizer, but the students will love you for it. Engaging their minds and enabling them to start learning is the goal of a successful teacher.

When I was going through Paramedic School and learning about cardiology, our instructor brought in a thirty-year veteran cardiologist from the hospital. He taught us a great deal about the heart, its functions, and cardiac health and disease. He was amazing, and he had an unmistakable passion for his subject. The class learned a lot from him, and he made the subject more interesting because of his passionate stories and enthusiasm. You want the learning to take place, and to do so, you need to find the right resources to do that. No one wants to sit through a "death by PowerPoint" lecture and listen to someone read off the screen with a monotone voice.

If finding a guest speaker is not a possibility, then I highly recommend you find something about the subject you find interesting. Make it your own. Remember this: you can make it as easy or as hard as you want. It is up to you!

Passion for a topic can go both ways. When I was teaching 11th-grade U.S. history, I spent a lot of time on the American Civil War. I thought the subject was fascinating, and I liked the time period. I loved everything about it, and I spent a lot of time discussing the politics involved in the decades leading up to the war, as well as the reconstruction and Jim Crow laws that followed. I thought the topic was interesting, and my students were reacting to the excitement and passion I showed in class. They learned a lot about the war and how it has shaped our culture and society today.

However, I spent so much time on the subject I was asked by my coworkers in the Social Studies Department about how I planned to get through all the other required material before the end of the semester. They were right to be concerned. In this case, my passion may have put a rush on other topics that were important as well. I had to make choices, and I had to use the remainder of my time wisely.

I decided what was relevant and what I could sum up and skip. Luckily, this was my decision to make, and I had the freedom to do so as a teacher. Our administration trusted me as a professional to get through the subject material and curriculum in the best way possible. No micromanagement was needed. I respected their trust and my freedom and worked very hard to do my best because of that trust. I learned a valuable lesson: not only did I need to find a passion for the subject, but I needed to do so promptly and not overlook other important parts of the curriculum.

You should be able to sense if the students understand and, if not, ask! Change what they are doing to make sure they grasp the concepts. A poor teacher will look up, or maybe not look up at all, and see blank stares from the students and just continue to get through what they intended for the day. For emergency service students preparing for Two Dark Thirty moments, this can be dangerous.

An engaging and caring teacher will go back to the beginning and try something different or new. Have the self-respect to take the time and ask questions of your students. Gage their understanding as you teach. Stop if there is a problem or confusion arises. At the end of the day, learning is contagious, but so is a misunderstanding. Be a storyteller and engage and captivate your students. Have faith in yourself and project a positive attitude. Set the tone and be the example you want them to follow. You are the class leader—the one who prepares them for the situations they'll face in the dark of the night.

Remember the moment, at Two Dark Thirty, when my partner and I were looking for a four-foot boa constrictor while trying to take care of a broken man? Keeping the attention of your students is like keeping a snake in its aquarium. As you use this chapter to improve your teaching style, you are ultimately preparing emergency service heroes and heroines to face the chaos that always ensues at Two Dark Thirty.

Mr. Hills Notes:
- Start by being a storyteller.

- Be engaging and use your senses to teach.

- Involve your students in learning. Have a plan to captivate your students.

- Consider bringing in a guest speaker!

- Mindset and attitude are everything.

- Be positive!

Low Angle Rope Rescue Training 2018. Training sign and vehicle placement located at the end of a parking area to advise local resident where training event was taking place. (Photo courtesy of the author)

Chapter Two

THE FUNDAMENTALS OF EDUCATION

"An investment in knowledge pays the best interest."
—*Benjamin Franklin*

When I was in my undergraduate program for secondary social studies education, I did my student-teaching practicum experience at a suburban high school in West De Pere, just outside of Green Bay Wisconsin.

My cooperating teacher (mentor) told me during our first meeting that on day two I would have all five-9th grade (freshman) World History classes. She would introduce me to the students and go through the course syllabus for the year and assign textbooks. After that they were all mine. There was no gradual introduction or taking over responsibility for one class a week and then two classes and so on, which was protocol for the university. Nope. "Sink or swim," she said. She also told me I could not use any of her instructional materials. I had to create all my own from scratch. I remember thinking, "Wow, I wish I had known this earlier." I managed to adapt and overcome. I spent all night trying to make sure I had enough material to work with for the first week.

In a way, she was right: "Either you can do this, or you can't." I was thrown into teaching and I was happy to do so. I learned a lot from her and I enjoyed my time at the school. The students were great and I even coached football. The important point is I had the confidence and the ability to correct my mistakes and learn from them. But I also had a great background and foundation to rest my abilities on. Let's start to explore these abbreviated formal education concepts.

What Is Curriculum?

"When I teach the formal curriculum, I have the chance to think about it ahead of time. I can rehearse it, I can illustrate it with self-deprecating humor and humble-sounding personal disclosure. I can try to make it come out just right."

— John Ortberg

When you start teaching, your school or organization should give you the curriculum for the course. Merriam-Webster's dictionary defines curriculum as:

(1) the courses offered by an educational institution. (2) a set of courses constituting an area of specialization.

Every state in the USA has a set curriculum for emergency services. Every college or school will have adopted a set of curricula from the state regulatory agency or administration. Some states even have defined curricula within their statutes or laws. Within the curriculum, there should be a list of the objectives, subject matter, lessons, and resources to be used. However, you may not have access to this information. Ask for it if you do not receive it right away.

The curriculum is nothing more than the course objectives and subject matter. In education, there are usually three different types of curricula: student-centered, subject-centered, or problem-centered. Often, the curriculum is directly related to national standards such as the National Fire Protection Association (NFPA) 1001 for the fire service, the US Federal Department of Transportation (USDOT), or the National Registry of EMTs (NREMT) for emergency medical services.

These national organizations create papers and documents that direct the scope of training. They create standards that the education and teaching must reflect. The textbook companies then take these standards and look for subject experts and national leaders to write the texts we use in our classrooms.

Colleges and public safety departments look at these texts and adopt their resources for the educational materials and courses they offer. Some colleges also employ course writers to create materials and course shells for their instructors, but many leave the course creation and writing to the full-time faculty members. Then, it is distributed to all the adjunct and associate instructors to disseminate the material in all the courses and classes.

The curriculum we see has gone through many steps and has taken many years to create. For instructors, it is there as a guide, so we know what to cover on this learning journey.

We need to understand the curriculum process and where we are taking our students. A good teacher will have investigated the curriculum and asked questions about where they should be guiding their students. Is the course you are teaching the culmination of the studies, or is it the beginning? What level of experience do your students come in with? What sorts of courses have your students had prior to your class, and what should they already know?

The curriculum is the path, but the teacher is the guide along the journey. To be a great guide, you should know where the potholes and bridges are along the path. You need to be familiar with the perils the students may face. It is your job to help them to have a successful learning experience and come out on the other side of the journey, ready to act in a professional manner.

Planning to Learn

"In preparing for battle, I have always found that plans are useless, but planning is indispensable."
—*President Dwight D. Eisenhower (General ret.)*

So, what exactly is a lesson plan? There are many types and many versions of a lesson plan. In the end, it is as simple as it sounds. It is a written document that has a basic outline of what you intend to teach for that day or for the course. It's usually only a page or less in length.

The lesson plan is important because it is your map of instruction. The plan is the recipe for how you propose to teach for the day. Without a plan, you are flying by the seat of your pants, and you can only handle that for so long. Trust me, I know. I've had times when I did not have a plan and was thrown into the fire of teaching without having prepped or looked at a thing. Luckily for me, I can ad-lib and ramble and talk about concepts and ideas while I review items from the book. It is not comfortable, and it is not fun. Do yourself a favor and have a written plan of action ready to go.

You should write out your lesson plan, both for the day and for the entire course. I have example lesson plans and templates on my website. In general, lesson plans have several factors to them. Here are some of the common items found within:

- **Lesson Goal:** *What do you expect the student to learn in the lesson itself, such as understanding the importance of a topic?*

- **Lesson Objectives:** *What should the student be able to accomplish after the lesson? Objectives can be as simple as learning to tie a knot a certain way or being able to explain the differences between two items.*

- **Instructor information:** *These are the items the teacher needs to know to successfully complete the lesson.*

- **Resources:** *These are physical items or copies of materials needed.*

- **Methodology:** *This includes the types of learning styles the instructor will incorporate, such as lectures, question/answer sessions, or hands-on activities.*

- **Aids:** *Aids are much like resources, but are specific to file names, such as PowerPoint files, etc.*

- **Evaluation:** *This is how the teacher plans to test the student's knowledge and achievement of the lesson. This can be a simple quiz or class demonstration.*

The lesson plan is also handy to have if you need a substitute for the day. Substitutes can see what you planned to do and your daily objectives. Administrators also like to see them if they do spot checks and walk-ins to see how you are doing as a teacher. In the end, they are for you and your benefit.

A lot of the textbook companies today have examples, and some even come with pre-arranged lesson plans. Like everything, though, you need to go through them and make them your own. If there is one thing I hope you get from reading my book, it is to avoid copying others and take ownership of your lesson plans. Create your own identity. Fit example lesson plans to meet your needs and your goals. Prepare yourself for success!

Educational Fundamentals

"Education is not preparation for life; education is life itself."
—*John Dewey*

As I said before, I intend this book to be a guide. I realize many in emergency services do not have formal training as teachers or in education. I've taken the instructor course and it is a decent rudimentary base, but sometimes more is needed. I've tried my best to condense what I have learned over the past twenty years as a teacher, so you can benefit from it.

There are a few basic educational concepts every teacher discovers when gaining their degree or certification. The classes on educational theory can be a bit arduous, lengthy, and thorough. You will most likely hear of, or might be expected to understand, the following major educational principles. I've tried to sum up the information the best I could while also getting to the main points of each theory quickly.

Maslow's Hierarchy of Needs

The first principle is Maslow's Hierarchy of Needs (2). This is a psychological concept created by Dr. A.H. Maslow. He authored a now-famous paper in 1943 entitled, '*A Theory of Human Motivation.*' In the paper, Maslow suggested there are five levels of needs that humans require to be positively motivated workers. The theory suggests we, as teachers, create the best learning environment when we acknowledge and ensure that these levels are met for our students. If we do not, then they may not learn adequately, or their learning will be impaired.

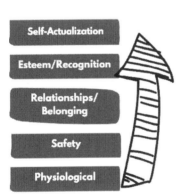

The base level is physiological needs. This level has basic requirements for survival, like water, food, and shelter. Once those are met, students can move on to safety and feel secure in their environment. They have a job or purpose.

Relationships and belonging are next, followed by esteem and recognition of your purpose and work.

Figure 1: Maslow's Hierarchy of Needs Flow Chart

Finally, the top level includes self-actualization, in which the person has become all they can be and have worked to become.

As an educator, you should strive to meet all five of these levels within your course to ensure your students succeed. Remember, these aspects are sometimes hard to recognize. Items like food and shelter are out of your reach or control. You should be in a room structure, but obviously not provide sleep or clothing. Safety should be easy for you to ensure. Nearly all schools or agencies have and require some sort of badge, code, or entry door access to where you will be teaching. This is also a bit outside of your responsibilities, but as a teacher, ensure the class environment is conducive to learning. Make sure there are no bullies or other feelings of resentment or anger in the room.

Belonging can be as simple as creating the team atmosphere, which I will cover in length later in the book. Esteem is well within your control as the instructor. Give praise and show respect to your students. Celebrate successes and learn from failures together.

Finally, aid in self-actualization. At the end of your course, you should see your students have achieved all you intended or more. The student should feel confident in what they have learned and in their new skills.

As you create your lesson plans, think about how you can achieve all five levels in your instruction.

Gardner's Multiple Intelligences

Our second major theory deals with how our students think. This relates to the types of activities and learning styles you will encounter in class. Your lesson plan should include the different learning activities you intend to use. There are many distinctive styles and learning types. Take a second and do a self-evaluation. Think about the following questions: *How do I like to learn? What makes a class interesting to me? What types of learning activities did I enjoy in school?*

In 1983, Dr. Howard Gardner first developed a theory on the relationships between the mind and learning in his book titled '*Frames of Mind.*' He later formulated the common styles of intelligence or ways people learn, called '*Tapping into Multiple Intelligences*' (3). His original theory named six types of learners, but over the years, it has expanded to include nine types.

1. *Linguistic*

2. *Musical*

3. *Kinesthetic*

4. *Spatial*

5. *Inter-personal*

6. *Intra-personal*

7. *Mathematical-Logic*

8. *Naturalistic*

9. *Existential*

The basis of the theory still rests on the fact there are three central core learning styles. Some people love reading books (visual learning); others, like myself, prefer to watch videos or listen to audio (auditory learners). Still, others learn best by using their hands (physical or kinesthetic learning). As educators, it is important to remember we are all different people, and we all have comfort zones for learning.

Learning is easiest when we are engaged. For example, sometimes I can sit and read a book for hours and not remember anything I just read. Was I bored? What happened to all the time? Some of the problem is attention, and some of it is whether I am tired, but a lot of the trouble has to do with whether I found the information interesting.

As a teacher, it is difficult, and always challenging, to find new ways to portray information to your students, especially if they have different learning preferences and styles than your own. It is your task to take these different types of learning styles and try to find ways of incorporating them into the lesson. Change things up. Make it interesting.

Think about the self-evaluation questions I asked you earlier. Your lesson should have at the very least the three core learning styles found in it. There should be a visual, auditory, and physical component to the lesson. How you achieve this is up to you. Have a short video segment, pair up and read a short story about the topic, and have a demonstration tool the students can use, touch, and feel. Whatever it is, if you hit all three of those basic core learning components, not only will you teach for all the learning types, but you will change up the routine of the class and keep things moving and interesting for your students.

Bloom's Taxonomy

A third major concept you may hear or be expected to understand is Bloom's Taxonomy (4). This is another educational theory developed by educational psychologist Benjamin Bloom in 1956. His theory contends it is not the instruction on how students learn that is important, but rather how the students think. Bloom suggested there are six different cognitive levels that will lead the student to competence in the subject.

Within Bloom's 1956 paper (4), he described the six cognitive levels as:

1. *Remembering (copying, defining, listening, outlining, and memorizing)*

2. *Understanding (annotation, summarizing, paraphrasing, and contrasting)*

3. *Applying (articulating, examining, implementing, and interviewing)*

4. *Analyzing (categorizing, breaking down, organizing, and questioning)*

5. *Evaluating (arguing, testing, assessing, and criticizing)*

6. *Creating (collaborating, devising, writing, and mixing)*

Just like Maslow, Bloom's levels begin at one level and move upward to six, which is the highest point of cognitive function for the student.

Think about it like elementary or grade school. As a five-year-old in kindergarten, you remember and learn the ABCs and 123s. You look at primary colors or basic shapes. It is all about simple remembering. Then you move to 1st grade, where you remember reading words and sight words. We start basic math with adding and subtracting. You graduate to 2nd grade, where you apply multiple-step processes and look at an overall picture. Expanding our reading comprehension and involving basic scientific concepts. Then, in 3rd grade, you analyze the ingredients of the cookie and think about how many chocolate chips are really in the whole box. Moving to 4th grade, you evaluate why people react the way they do at the lunch line or at recess. Social skills are realized and thought about. Finally, you get to fifth grade and your teacher asks you to work with other students and show them how to do something like you just did, to demonstrate and teach.

Obviously, those are just simple examples, but the basic concept is evident. The different thinking patterns work their way up in complexity, time, and experience. Think about how your our own teachers, over the years, have used these principles to help you learn. How can you incorporate them into your own lessons? How can you create an educational environment to incorporate these higher levels of skill and application? How can you challenge your students to achieve more and apply more?

KISS Method

One of the best methods teachers have used for decades is the KISS method. The term means "Keep it Simple, Stupid," but has evolved to a more politically correct and friendly version: "Keep it Super Simple." It is a pneumonic reminder, as a teacher, that you do not have to complicate your activities and lessons just to make things harder and more complex. How many classes have you had where the instructor droned on about the course and explained what you were about to do, only to look around the room at the other blank faces and slowly raise your hand and say, "So what now?" As the leader in the room, it is up to you to define what the educational goals are and how to achieve them. Don't overcomplicate for the sake of making it complicated.

Keeping your lesson plan and the goals of the day super simple will also help you as the instructor. If you make things hard and complex, you will be promising yourself a lifetime of endless explanations to your students. Making it difficult sometimes does have its benefits and challenges the students--but on an everyday basis, KISS.

When I first started teaching at the high school level, there was a new English teacher down the hall from me. He was young and full of energy. He had an "I'll prove to them how smart I am" mentality and attitude. He carried himself as a professor and well-to-do, and he set the educational bar extremely high, almost impossibly high, for his students. He started the year off by requiring two different book reports in the first month of school. The reports had to be in APA (American Psychological Association) format and needed to be at least ten pages in length. He thought he would challenge the students.

What happened over the course of a few months did not surprise me. His students revolted against him, he lost control, and his classroom was a nightmare. He went from a high-energy professor to a barely dragging, sullen individual, and he quit at the end of the first semester. He didn't use KISS. He thought if he made things complicated, complex, and impossible the students would try harder. Having high expectations and making things in your class difficult and challenging are two different things.

It is imperative to communicate with your students. Tell them what you want to see them do, while also encouraging them and pushing them to get there. Challenge your students, obviously, but also focus on what you want to achieve in the class and where you want the students to end up. Take the time to plan out the lesson in the best, most efficient way possible. Use the KISS method to think about what your plan is and how you plan to succeed. Keeping it super simple will also help you keep your lessons on track and will be easier for you to follow. As you communicate the plan, you show your students you care, and that you are willing to help them get to the finish line.

SMART Goals

Goal setting, by the students themselves, is a more recent addition to education. This has been attempted in many ways, such as keeping a portfolio of students' coursework to be graded at the end of the class and show their work improvement. Other methods include having a non-graded essay paper or having the student explain the main concepts that were covered in class to determine their competency and to demonstrate improvement.

SMART goals stand for: Specific, Measurable, Achievable, Relevant, and Time-bound. The concept allows students to choose their goal to evaluate their chosen benchmark for success in a project or for a class.

All the specifics would need to be written out, and each concept should have a definite explanation. The biggest takeaway from this kind of educational philosophy is the fact the student takes ownership and selects the goal or goals they wish to improve upon. The fact the students choose the goals for themselves has an advantage over a teacher-selected evaluation.

The largest issue I have ever had with SMART goals is getting the student to drill down and select a goal that meets all the targeted parts. Usually, they are too vague or are not measurable. However, SMART goals can have a great part in education as another tool in your teacher's toolbox. SMART goals are especially useful for hands-on tasks.

Crew Resource Management

One of the best examples of CRM (Crew Resource Management) is during a full code on a pulseless, non-breathing (PNB) cardiac arrest patient. In our department, when we respond to a cardiac arrest and the patient is pulseless and non-breathing, we respond with our ambulance of two members and our engine with two members. Our battalion chief will also respond if they are available to assist. The police department is also dispatched to the scene to assist with the family's needs or questions.

Using CRM principles, we train our crew to work as a team. We often call this the 'pit crew' mentality. We use the concept that everyone has a specific job function. We work in tandem and together in our various roles, such as: lead medic, cardio-pulmonary resuscitation (CPR) manual compressions or our mechanical assist device, bag valve mask (BVM) or airway, intravenous (IV) access and medication administration, note-taker, and monitor management. We all have defined roles and we all have defined parameters to work under. This crew mentality allows us to concentrate and focus instead of trying to do more than one thing at a time. We use this system effectively and efficiently.

So, where did this system come from?

The origins began in the airline industry with a concept called CRM. David Beaty, in 1969, wrote a paper entitled, '*The Human Factor in Aircraft Accidents.*' His paper argued it was the human factor that led to poor situational awareness and to the devastating loss of life. Human factors often led to incidents where the pilots failed to work together to troubleshoot the issues and challenges they were facing. They ultimately chose against using their equipment and tried to figure it out on their own. CRM principles employ the strategy that teamwork is the only answer. This is achieved through communication, leadership, cooperation, and decision-making.

This is a concept you will encounter in the emergency services field and should teach to your students. The situational awareness factor is obviously huge in our industry, and it is imperative the students realize they will need to depend on others to have a successful outcome. I'll talk more about teamwork later in the book.

Knowledge, Skills, and Abilities

*"Knowledge has to be improved, challenged,
and increased constantly, or it vanishes."*
—*Peter Drucker*

KSA is a very common acronym you will see in emergency services education. The knowledge, skills, and abilities (KSA) model employs a stepping stone base level of knowledge, taught by didactic instruction or book learning. This foundation of the pyramid is the largest component and takes a great deal of time and energy to disseminate. The coursework for the student is based on the job or position they will be training for. So, in the instance of a firefighter or paramedic, they will be in the classroom learning all there is about the bookwork and knowledge of the position. Once they have shown mastery or assessed a high enough level of understanding, they will be upgraded to the skills portion, the next step.

Within the skills section, the student will learn the hands-on tactile movements and assignments that come with the position. This is where the repetition and muscle memory centers come into play. The skills employed will be those they are expected to be able to do at Two Dark Thirty with no sleep, in the dark, and with their gloves on. Examples of these skills could be how to catch a hydrant, basic forceable entry techniques, IV starts, 12-lead placement, radio reports, and other more basic abilities. During this step of training, students expand their base knowledge and ideally show the incorporation of the knowledge with the skills, demonstrating how to use the new information.

The final and most important stone is ability. This step of training shows the student has learned the knowledge, understands the skills involved in being successful, and now needs to practice the ability to do the job. This is a higher learning level that shows not only the adaptation of the prior education but the ability to apply knowledge to perform a task. The mastery of the knowledge, the skills, and the ability to perform successfully in a specific role is the essence of the KSA model.

OODA Loop

Colonel John Boyd of the U.S. Air Force authored the 1976 paper 'Destruction and Creation' for fighter pilots. He details the OODA Loop mechanism in his writing. This acronym stands for: Observe, Orient, Decide, Act, and then loop back to observe and repeat the process. Col. Boyd found that fighter pilots were having trouble with dog fights (attacking enemy aircraft) and dying because they were not using their senses to become situationally aware. He recognized the situations they face are time sensitive and have a huge component of reaction time and split-second thinking. To slow down the fight-or-flight psychology of our minds, he argued that we need to train our minds. His creation was OODA Loop mental processing also called the Boyd Cycle. This system was fully dynamic and would quicken responses as the students were forced to use the system. Boyd argued that the goal was to become so aware that you would not have to think about the orient and decide steps and go straight to act because you are fully aware of the situation and possible solutions. In emergency situations, we must slow the situation down, step back, and realize we have time to think and act.

This concept of situational awareness for our incident commanders and crew leaders has been embraced by several fire departments, and it is now moving into the EMS field. It's an additional tool in your toolbox you can use to teach your students about decision-making, assessing what you've done, and evaluating what needs to be modified to accomplish the mission and produce positive results. The term serves as another simple mental prompt to help us remember we must assess our situation before making a decision and acting upon it.

Bell Work

When I was teaching middle school, I used a system called 'Bell Work', created by Dr. Harry Wong in his book, '*First Days of School.*' He talked about using this type of reinforced learning as a review tool. The 'bell work' questions were short--only five questions. I had them on the board as my students entered the room, just prior to class beginning.

On the first day, I explained to my students the significance, the reasoning, and my expectations for the bell work. It is always imperative to set the bar and explain why you set the bar where it is.

Communication is at the forefront of anything you do, whether you are a teacher or a leader. So, I walked the students through the 'bell work' activity on day one. I explained to them the process and that the questions would come from the prior day's learning, the reading materials, and the notes they took. Sometimes it was a map they needed to identify locations on. Other times, it was a timeline they had to interpret and place dates on in the correct order. They could use all their reference materials, but I also wanted them to write the questions down and use them as a study guide for future exams. I always used 'bell work' questions on the tests.

The students knew the routine. Every day, they came into the room, sat down, and got to work. It was a great reinforcement tool that worked extremely well for me. It not only started the class off on the right foot, but it also enabled me free time to take attendance and to get any other materials ready while the students were busy for the first five minutes of class.

I did the same thing when I taught college-level courses to adults. I have found that to be successful, you need to develop a routine. People love freedom, but they also love knowing what to expect. Routines set the students up for success because they are familiar with what you expect them to achieve in the class. The routine is the basis for where they will go for the day, and they will understand why you are asking them to do it. It is comforting to know what to expect. This expectation gives students the ability to relax and have an enjoyable learning environment. Think about how you would like the class to be organized.

Using Evaluations

Evaluation is not a bad thing. It is the only way we can ever change what went wrong and figure out what we need to do to overcome our obstacles and conquer our challenges. The purpose of an evaluation is to gauge your students' learning. Evaluations will become one of your best friends. They are a tool every teacher uses to test the knowledge of every student.

However, every teacher must take this with a grain of salt. Some students excel at taking tests, and there is a science to test-taking. Some students get horrible anxiety and freeze up. Others are not terrific readers and possibly have reading comprehension issues. Any evaluation you use or create should have multiple types of questions. You should try not to give an essay-only or multiple-choice-only exam. Each evaluation should be a combination of all kinds of different types of questions. This goes back to Gardner's Multiple Intelligences. This will give those with multiple learning styles the chance to excel at a set of questions. In this way, you will be able to give an adequate evaluation of the didactic (book) learning.

A physical and hands-on evaluation must also be done in the emergency services profession. There are many aspects of being a first responder that cannot be tested with a pencil. Some, like bedside manner, can only be observed. Still, others are time-sensitive, such as a turn-out drill. Your course should incorporate these types of hands-on kinesthetic learning evaluations and activities. In my experience as a firefighter, I have found nearly all prefer this method rather than sitting and listening to lectures and group projects. Most want to get their hands dirty and get into the use of the tool or scenario. A great teacher will incorporate all these multiple types, understand their proper use, and time them within the curriculum.

Once you have established your evaluations and have used them, a great teacher will look at the data. I always go through my tests and look for mistakes and common questions the students missed.

1. *I ask myself if the question was worded poorly.*

2. *Did the available answers not make sense? Or was there more than one choice that was too similar?*

3. *Did I not cover the material in the way I expected?*

4. *Did the students misunderstand some of the important topics?*

5. *I look for trends and for holes in the evaluation. Did a large percentage all get question #12 wrong, or did everyone have the same wrong answer for a fill-in-the-blank?*

There is always something to improve for the next time. Every good evaluation will be updated and will be changed to be better.

If you are an instructor, and you are still using the same tests and quizzes as last year or the past decade, I implore you to evaluate your spirit and effort. I've seen some instructors still using the old blue ditto copy (a unique early-generation copy machine that used blue ink) for exams from the early 1990s. It is amazing they have such low standards or esteem for themselves. The evaluations you have been using are not perfect, and there is always room to change.

Ask a colleague to look at your work to see if they can find flaws or corrections. Much like having someone else proofread your paper or manuscript. You may know what you want, but it may not come out the way you intend. If all your students are failing to attain mastery in one aspect of your class, ask why that is. What needs to be improved? As I've said before, you need to own your own mistakes and learn from them. Evaluate yourself and your teaching style and make continual improvements. Always remember, as a teacher, you are also a lifelong learner. It is a journey without an end because there is always something new to understand and adapt to.

Quizzing for Competence

Typically, every probationary firefighter gets assigned a field training officer (FTO) or preceptor, someone to train them more closely for the first month of their time in the department. I enjoy this role. Once, I was assigned a probationary firefighter, Mike. Mike came to our department with full-time experience, having served on a few prior departments, yet I believed he needed some additional training, specifically with medications in the ambulance. I felt this way because of his hesitation when I asked him to tell me about some medications we carry.

I was uncomfortable with his lack of knowledge of the medications. We worked together; we were partners in the ambulance, and I needed to know he had my back, and I had his. I needed to trust that he knew what he was doing, because when times get tough, we were alone together until more help came. Trust is key.

Every day when I was checking off the ambulance in the morning, making sure all the tools, equipment, and materials we needed were in stock and ready to go, I challenged Mike, "Hey, what's in the fridge?"

As his preceptor, I assessed him every day. I asked him what the medication was, what the correct dose was, and in what medical emergencies would we choose to give it. It took Mike a month to get it right—but day after day, time after time, we worked together to achieve the end goal.

Daily quizzing is not a dreadful thing, and it is never a bad option to reinforce information. Sometimes you just need to memorize things and put them in your thick gray brain matter. Frequent repetition builds the memory recall centers in the brain, so you can access information even in the dead of night and in the most stressful of situations. It's essential for those Two Dark Thirty times.

To build confidence in your people, don't hesitate to quiz them daily about everything you want them to know. Having the ability to do both good and harm as a paramedic is a great privilege. It is possible to cause harm, and even death, if you don't know what you are doing. I do not want anyone to be put in that position. Emergency service personnel should recall the information like the back of their hand. When seconds count, they need to be able to remember the information off the top of their heads, regardless of the time of night or if they've been running calls all day, or if they only had a half-hour to an hour of sleep. The public community expects emergency service heroes to know what they're doing when they come to aid in crisis situations.

Lastly, don't hesitate to do the deeper dive. Explain the importance of what we do and how we do it, especially to new students. You may even find that these conversations draw in veteran members, who enjoy telling their tales and how they learned from the job.

Formal quizzing is only one type of evaluation and reinforcement of learning. Quizzes have their place as an evaluation tool and are extremely important. The consistent use of quizzes reinforces the learned material for the student. The hope is they can recall the information more readily, use the information to further learn, and allow it to become a steppingstone to expand their knowledge. Quizzes keep the students up-to-date and shows them what they should know and understand. It keeps them on their toes. This will also give you the opportunity to gauge their knowledge and comprehension.

Quizzes must be short, though. They are not final exams or tests. They should be simple and easy to both grade and read quickly. I recommend five to ten questions that are specific to the purpose. You should also make the questions easy to understand and comprehend. They should not require major research. The student's answers should simply recall the needed information.

Here are the questions I asked Mike each morning shift:

1. *What three medications do we keep in the fridge?*

2. *What are the doses for each medication?*

3. *Why do we give these medications?*

4. *What are three side effects of these medications?*

5. *Why do we keep these medications in the refrigerator?*

These five simple questions did not leave any doubt about what I intended them to mean. Each question had a specific answer that could be recalled at Two Dark Thirty. They were short, sweet, and to the point.

A good teacher wants to help the student learn the information in any way they can. They will make numerous attempts to relay the information. As a teacher, you will see that we all learn differently, and we are all unique. You will have to continuously monitor and adjust the style of teaching to help get to the point and deliver the subject material to diverse groups of students. Coming up with various ways to distribute the information to many different types of people is part of the fun of being a teacher, and it is also one of the most challenging. As your experience grows, you will see how you can explain the same material in numerous different ways, multiple times, within the same class.

Creative or Constructive Criticism

With critiques, the teacher is to be positive and yet still provide valuable feedback on the student's work. Your suggestions to improve the student's work must be specific.

Critiques can be provided effectively using the common sandwich method, which employs a positive comment, followed by a negative comment, followed finally by a positive comment. Sandwiching the negative comments between two positive comments diminishes the potential impact of the negative. This method is employed to lighten the load of the critique.

The sandwich method is only a possibility. Your techniques should depend on your students and how they respond to feedback. Some will just want you to be honest and open.

Any kind of feedback or criticism is meant to help the student discover where their flaws are. Some students will see the error in their ways, while others need it to be pointed out. Regardless, the feedback should always be directed at their work, and it should always be followed up with a way to improve the work. Never tell a student they are wrong without offering suggestions on how they can improve.

Let's Put This Together

I had a chemistry professor in college who lectured to a large room of hundreds of students. He would literally stand on stage with four overhead projectors. Each one of the projectors had a different page of notes. For an hour and a half, he went from projector to projector, reading the notes. He stood facing the screens and never once turned around. The hundreds of us in the lecture room just barely had enough time to copy down the notes he read before he would slap up the next page of notes and move on to the next projector. We learned nothing about chemistry.

From my point of view, the lecture was a major waste of time. No one paid attention to what he was saying, nor could they comprehend it. The students were left to come up with their own study groups, teach themselves, and try their best to learn the information. There may be those that think the professor was empowering us to achieve more, but was he?

There are ways to achieve this as a teacher, but the way he went about it was unsuccessful. Although I passed Chemistry Lab, I still have a three-credit F on my transcripts from failing Chem Lecture. Coincidentally, that professor was removed from the university shortly thereafter for his high student failure rate and his lack of attention to being an educational professor rather than a researcher.

Do not be this kind of teacher. You must change things up in your class. Remember why you are there: to engage students in the learning process, so they will be prepared and attentive during their Two Dark Thirty moments.

Before you begin the didactic phase of your instruction (meaning the lecture and book portion), try starting off with a question-and-answer session, or even a joke or media snippet of something funny. Break the ice. Get everyone relaxed and ready to learn.

Always remember, your presentation needs to be adjusted for different learning styles, according to Gardner. Part of your explanation can be in PowerPoint or lecture note form, but only a part. Not all. Do not lecture and do note-taking for the entire class. Change to a question-and-answer on what you just lectured. Be prepared with your own five to ten questions if no one has any for you! The questions should be ones that someone who was listening could answer quickly.

Then move on to a short video, or other illustrations, of the same topics. This type of multimedia use will ensure you are involving all types of learners. This reinforces the learning and gives you a glimpse into whether your message was received or not. If not, stay on course and go through it again until everyone is on the same page.

Do not go on and tell your students it is up to them to make up the difference. That is your job. If you were too confusing and lost your students, you need to own that and pick up at the start again. Adapt and change. Remember, your students come first!

Now you are hitting different memory centers in the brain. Tie the lecture to the video or illustrations. Talk about how they relate. Then, after some time, go through some more brief questions and answers. Again, be prepared for your topic and have notes made for yourself.

Finally, go through it hands-on, with samples or experiences. Let students handle it, work with it, take it apart, move it, and possibly break it, especially in the fire service.

Having done multiple types of lecturing, watching, and demonstrating ties all three aspects together. Repeat that sequence over and over. Every day, come back to class and ask the same couple of questions until everyone gets them right. Change things up and keep the students on their toes. Take time to explain why it is important and how it relates to the success of whatever it is you want to have them memorize.

Remember Bloom. Communicate! Do this over the next few classes and you will be impressed with your student's understanding and recall.

A sample timeline might be:

Day 1 - Overview of the subject, expectations, a short video or illustration, and a hands-on activity.

Day 2 - Review with a question-and-answer session, go over the material again, go over the next steps, and do hands-on practice.

Day 3 - Consists of a quiz on the material covered, a group activity, and a hands-on demonstration of how the item works.

Once you have set up an educational and instructive pattern to use and have modeled the behavior, don't hesitate to break it down and let others from within your class do the teaching. This is especially true when you have a subject genius in your course. Encourage the students who you feel are good at communication or the ones that are masters of a subject to 'help you' by instructing the course. By sharing the wealth and the burden of teaching, you are showing we are all in this together, we all have strengths, and we all have something to contribute.

You may also find diamonds in the rough who end up being natural leaders. Student-teachers can become a confident resource and assistant who will move your class forward. By encouraging and sharing experiences, you are doing your job both as a teacher and as a leader. You are developing and expanding the students you have, helping people realize their potential and preparing emergency management heroes for Two Dark Thirty.

Mr. Hills Notes:

- The curriculum will help you know where to go.

- Have multiple types of learning activities ready.

- Review and repeat the information.

- Learning with your students is okay!

- Be open and ready to answer questions.

- Encourage others to participate and teach.

- Have realistic expectations of your students.

- Use evaluation to improve your class and yourself.

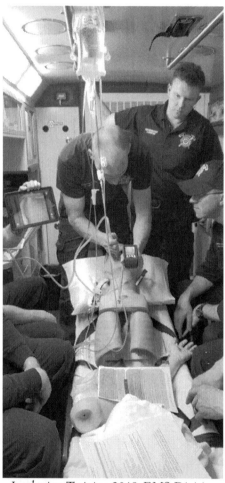

Intubation Training 2019. EMS Division Chief, Jared Thompson, is instructing on the use and technique of a video laryngoscope during intubation attempts in back of ambulance. (Photo courtesy of the author)

Chapter Three

How to Be a Successful Teacher

"Opportunity is missed by most because it is dressed in overalls and looks like work."
—*Thomas Edison*

Becoming a public school teacher requires some time to observe other teachers and how they operate. I spent a few days in the 8th-grade classroom of an English teacher. He was an elderly gentleman with huge bushy white eyebrows and an obvious comb-over that was not fooling anyone. He was gaunt and had a slight bend in his posture from age. His thirteen-year-old students were well-behaved, and when the bell rang, they quietly walked in and sat down. Not a single student spoke or fooled around. The old-fashioned man gradually shuffled to the front of the room and began to write on his green chalkboard.

I was shocked by all of this. I simply could not believe what I was seeing. The 8th graders were not only being respectful of this teacher but doing the work he asked of them without a hassle. I thought it must be me—I must be influencing them to behave in the class just by sitting in the back. (On a side note, this is called the Observer or Hawthorne Effect.) After I had been there a few days, I stopped one of the students after class and asked them if the class always acted this way. She said, "Well, yes. We like him, and we respect him. "

What made this classroom so well-behaved? The setting was obviously one that was conducive to learning. It was organized and neat, with everything in its place. There were classic examples of correct grammar posters on the walls, as well as a bulletin board with students' work that was high quality and award-winning, but the most special thing in the room was the teacher, the elder statesman. It was his presence and demeanor. He came in with an aura of compassion and a kind spirit, like a grandpa. Everyone wanted to do a great job for him. They didn't want to let him down or disappoint him. His classroom itself didn't really have much to do with it, beyond what he portrayed to his students: his expectations.

His presence and demeanor were strict, and he enforced his rules appropriately. He didn't accept misbehavior, the usual middle school hijinks. I asked him how he was able to control the students so well. What was the secret? He stated the students knew what the expectations were, and they knew and understood the rules. "Tell them how to behave and they will follow you." His classroom was inviting, secure, warm, and had the sense of history and nostalgia of an old library. The environment made students want to learn.

Formal Classroom

Where is a classroom found? Is it in a building? Is it in the multi-million-dollar training facility? On the kitchen table? Or is it on the street?

The correct answer is yes. It is everywhere and can be found at any time. A formal classroom can take the shape of any situation or be in any physical location. It is any place where you can have a teachable moment and learn a lesson. A classroom can be as simple as a place where you set an example and demonstrate how to tie a rope or knot properly. It could be in the back of the ambulance with a patient. Or it could be in the basement of a building. In this service, the classroom can take many shapes and sizes. The important parts are who the instructor is and who the students are.

The formal classroom is only an abstract idea of where learning can take place. I have taught in some massive and expensive classrooms full of mind-blowing technology, and I have also taught in storage rooms. Was the learning or my method of instruction different? Yes, and no. I used, or at least tried to use, the technology that I had access to, to the best of my abilities, but teaching and learning do not require elaborate technology. It can make things easier, especially when you are trying to differentiate your learning activities, but in the end, the formal classroom can be anywhere and everywhere you are. Look around; it might be where you are right now.

The classroom is just a concept of reality. The important idea you should understand is that the classroom is anywhere that learning can take place. It should be open and safe where the students can absorb the content and apply the knowledge. Ensure that you have that environment established.

Classroom Management

Classroom management (CM) is a simple concept, but it can often be the most challenging for new teachers. CM directly deals with you as an instructor. How you present yourself and how you communicate your rules, expectations, and beliefs will directly influence your CM. There are certain types of styles you can strategize with. Whether you want to be autocratic-authoritarian, laissez-faire, or diplomatic, any style you choose has its own set of positives and negatives.

Authoritarians tend to be rigid and demanding, with little group work or talking allowed. These tend to be the classical model classrooms. "Laissez-faire" is French for "allow to do." This style allows the students to talk and interact with each other very frequently. The class is open to people walking around and freely thinking and challenging themselves. Diplomatic or democratic styles tend to mix the two extremes, allowing students to interact with a set figurehead or group moderator. They allow the students to have a say in the instruction method.

The type of style you choose also depends on the class you are teaching. If you are instructing a class that has high-risk involvement, like confined space or high-angle rope rescue, you want to be more authoritative and in charge. But if the class is more focused on didactic and lecturing, then you can have more of a laissez-faire and diplomatic touch with discussion and explanations allowing the students to learn freely.

When I was teaching middle school 7th-grade geography, I always started the year as a tyrant and authoritarian. I put the fear of God in those kids! They were young, and as middle schoolers, they were at the age where they wanted to sow their oats. I felt I needed a heavy hand and needed to make sure I started the year off with a bang.

It was easy for me. Being six foot two and weighing two hundred fifty pounds, I can bark like a drill sergeant and will grab your attention whether you like it or not. I took the approach that I could not sit back and have a lazy attitude, or my middle school classroom would go off the walls and out of control. Teachers who started off that way were in for a long and tough year, but those who started off hard and rigid could always ease up as students earn increased responsibility.

Like 7th graders, most adults can be the same. People often say they hate the rules and want freedom, but I have found that freedom, like respect, is earned.

Regardless of which style you use, be sure to communicate your expectations and rules. Time and time again, we see the best organizations have set policies and beliefs that are known by all. Staff who work at these organizations understand what they must do.

Organizations that have little to no rules or are ever-changing are places where most people look for the door to find a way out of there as soon as possible. No one wants to deal with ever-changing directions and expectations.

Make sure your rules for your class are in the syllabus and go through them with your students on day one. Read them together, give examples, and answer questions. Three months in is not the place for people to ask why you expect something done a certain way. Everyone should be on the same page from day one. If they are not, it is your fault as the teacher and leader of the class. Be the leader and communicate with them!

Participate in the Lesson

"Tell me and I forget. Teach me and I remember. Involve me and I learn."
—Ben Franklin

Learn by teaching, letting students help, and letting students learn by doing.

When you want to really know a subject or remember more about it, you need to teach it to someone else. Just the act of explaining a topic to someone else will cement in your mind the little things and the more complex ideas about the topic. By taking the time to explain something to someone, you activate multiple receptors in your brain, and you retain more. Simply put, you learn by teaching.

You should research your topic and become acquainted with the subject if you are not familiar with it already. No, you do not need to know everything from top to bottom about the subject, but you do need to have a very good grasp of the material in question. You should have enough knowledge about the matter to answer questions about the times, topics, people, and events. However, you should also know enough about it to suggest or show students where they could find more information. Another way to look at this is you should know enough to be dangerous.

When I was in graduate school, I had a professor who split the entire course into different topics, with all the information broken down week by week. On the first day of class, he split the students into groups and then assigned us weeks and topics. He explained our job was to teach the students about the topic for that week. At first, I thought it was a load of bull, and that this high-paid professor was just trying to get away with not doing anything. However, as time went on, I realized we were all learning more because we were taking the information to heart. Not only were we paying more attention, because every week a different group was presenting the information in different ways, but we were all in competition to outdo the prior group. We wanted to be the best, and we wanted our topic week to blow the minds of the other students in the class.

We all learned far more by doing this than just sitting there, listening, and writing notes. This is active learning and active teaching. You always learn more by doing and by explaining the process to someone else. This happens because you are forced to break down the information and come up with a way to give that information to another person. This is the teaching challenge! It is hard to do, especially if you want to do it well.

I have come to realize there is no such thing as being a true expert, so do not think you must know it all. No one does.

On a side note, if someone tells you that you're expected to know everything, pack your things, and say goodbye, because that is not a place you want to be working at, for, or doing business with. Those are completely unrealistic thoughts and expectations that do nothing but set people up for failure.

Remember who your audience is, their age group, and their experience, and coordinate your expectations with the audience's level. For example, kindergarteners who can barely read and write should never be expected to know all the states and capitals of the USA, but college postgraduates should know how to write an APA (American

Psychological Association) style paper with correct notations and references. Even if they may not remember how to do so, they would be experienced enough to find the answers on their own.

Even in an emergency management class, a good teacher will know the audience, including their experiences. Good teachers understand how to communicate with that group, and they adapt their programs to fit the situation and the learning levels of their students by creating inventive ways to participate in the learning.

Dependability

"Your word is your bond," as the old adage goes. What it comes right down to are some simple questions that everyone will ask themselves about you.

1. *Can you be trusted?*

2. *Do you have honor?*

3. *What kind of integrity do you have?*

4. *Are you the right person to carry a problem or issue to?*

5. *Will you do what you say?*

6. *Are you trustworthy?*

7. *Can people count on your loyalty?*

Whatever question we ask, it comes down to a cold simple fact, especially in the emergency services: can I trust you with my life?

Dependability is also important in the teaching realm. What people think of you and how they look at you are aspects of the job that you must face every day. Your students see you as the leader of the class. They need to know you are dependable and able to follow through on your word and in your management style. Students will seek you out if they trust you. Your coworkers will seek your advice and counsel if they know you can be dependable and honest. Looking the part of a teacher and having a positive attitude are the beginning. You need to follow through on what you say and show that you mean it. Dependability is something that is illustrated over time. It is a pattern that is seen by those watching.

How do you want others to look at you as an instructor? Do you want people to see you as a knowledgeable and go-to person? Do you want them to see you and think you have it together and you know what you are doing? What you say you will do matters. If you promise to grade and provide feedback on time, then do it. No excuses. Do the right thing, be responsible and be a person of your word, because the students are depending on you. Your reputation depends on your dependability.

Be Flexible but Firm

If the students cannot turn in the assignment on the appropriate day, then it will be late. You should have a policy for late work and most colleges will have rules for such, but if they do not, here are some examples that have worked for me. These policies provided some flexibility yet also maintained an expected structure.

One policy idea is all assignments turned in after one day are 10% off, and 10% off for every day after. No work is accepted after 5 days. There is understanding and flexibility in the policy, but it also shows work is to be turned in on time and promptly.

The world we live in is gray. It is not black and white. Life happens, and as instructors, we need to be able to adjust and move with our students. We want them to achieve. I would rather a student turn in something late that they attempted to learn from than turn in nothing at all. Having this type of policy shows this and is mandated by most educational institutions I have worked for.

If a student does poorly on an exam, I will give them the opportunity to get half of those points back. Usually, this will entail all question types, not just the essay or short-answer questions. They need to have access to their wrong answers, and they need to explain to me, in complete sentences on a separate document, why they got the question wrong, and what the correct answer would be, including the page number in the text where the information was found. This not only makes the student accountable but also reinforces the missed learning the student lacked prior to the exam. This also gives them the chance to resurrect some of the missed points They will still have a lower grade, but hopefully they will understand the material better, and on the next evaluation, they will understand how they should study.

Just because you provide this opportunity does not mean your students will take advantage of it. Some students will be happy with their grades, and others may not care too much. The option for them to achieve more is there. You may want to have a frank discussion with those who choose not to do it, because their attitude in class can reflect how they will react at Two Dark Thirty.

One other policy idea is to not accept any late work. This rarely works well, and it can create a negative, us-versus-them mentality atmosphere in your classroom.

Ultimately, it is up to you as the instructor. Good teachers want the students to learn, even if it is a few days later than desired. Having a policy for late work does not mean you want them to do all their work late. Establish the adequacy of your assignments. Clearly communicate the class expectations. Ensure there is no miscommunication and answer questions the students may have honestly and fairly. Be fair and firm, but be flexible.

Empathy and Compassion

In my first year of teaching 12th grade remedial U.S. history, I had a student that I was also coaching in football. He was a great kid and a very hard worker. I knew the hard life he lived growing up on a dairy farm, and I knew what his family expected of him. I gave him a bit more freedom because of this, and yet he still had all his assignments in and was missing no work. He was an excellent student and earned my respect.

One day in class, which was the first hour of the day, he fell asleep in the last five minutes. He sat in the back and stayed away from the other students. One of the other students raised her hand and asked why I always allowed him to fall asleep. Other students voiced their agreement and asked the same question. This woke him up, and he sat there in the back, saying nothing. I looked at him and I looked at the students. I asked him directly, "Why don't you tell the rest of the class what time you got up this morning?" He told them he got up at 3:00

AM. I asked him, "Why on Earth were you up so early?" He told the class he needed to milk the cows and get them all fed. If he wanted to play football after school, his father expected him to get all his chores done before school.

This eighteen-year-old student put in a day's work prior to coming to class. I asked the other students what time they woke up in the morning. None answered, and they all looked at the ground. I told them not to worry about other people or what other students were doing, but to worry about themselves. They got the message: do not judge another person, because you do not know what their story is. You cannot assume you know. Have empathy and try not to criticize.

On the flip side, sometimes the student chooses to fail. On rare occasions, students are not ready to learn, or they are not ready to be involved. Sometimes they don't study for the exam, or they forget an assignment or project We are all human. We have our bad days, we make mistakes, and we all fail ourselves, so there is room for flexibility. But we also have standards and expectations to uphold. As teacher, it is up to you to make sure everyone is on the same page. If you take ownership of your course and create a positive learning environment, nearly all issues will take care of themselves, and you will have empathy and compassion.

Now and then, you need a heavy hand or to be a rigid taskmaster. Learn the difference in styles and find an appropriate balance. It goes back to knowing your audience. You should understand where your students are coming from. I could have treated my student differently and been stricter with him. But what would it have achieved? Would he have been as successful in class?

As with most things in life, classroom situations are rarely black and white. Most of the time, they are varying shades of gray. It will be up to you, as the leader of the class, to organize and manage your students. Just remember your students are people too, not robots—and they will be the ones who need to be ready at Two Dark Thirty.

Your classroom management style will change depending on your student audience and the type of course. Always have a plan for action and always have accommodations ready to go. Be compassionate and have empathy for those who seek it.

Be a Prepper

"Before anything else, preparation is the key to success."
—Alexander Graham Bell

As a teacher, you are expected to come to class prepared for the lesson. Do not think you are knowledgeable enough to just walk in and start teaching off the top of your head. I have met a few teachers who could do it successfully. I have met some that think they are that good, and trust me when I tell you, they are not!

A teacher's main job, besides ensuring the students have an adequate safe learning environment, is communication and planning. You should be aware of the information for the day and know all the ins and outs of the lesson. Be able to answer questions as needed and to relate the lesson to real-life or real-world examples. You should be so familiar with the information in class that it enables you to have an aura and attitude that demonstrates you understand the topic.

Prepping for the class takes time. It may take you an hour to prepare for an hour class, or longer for even longer classes. I start my prepping with the textbook I will be using. Most books today come with their own lesson plans, activities, and tests. I like to go through it all and see what kinds of information they have provided from the textbook company. Sometimes it is fantastic, and everything is pristine and ready to go. But other times I have found little to nothing, and I have had to develop all my own materials from scratch. If this is the case, you do not want to find out the night before class. Prepping takes time, and you need to invest the appropriate amount of time in the book and materials before you teach it.

Prepare for the class the night before or a few days earlier. Schedules are hectic but take the time to set yourself up to be successful. Give yourself the best chance at being a knowledgeable teacher that the students want to see again. Be the teacher you'd like to take a class from.

Be prepared for class, have the material down, and be able to offer suggestions and different learning activities to reinforce the class information for the day. Once you have taught the class or course multiple times, you will likely find yourself changing things to make it better. Evaluate the activities and find new material to keep yourself and the course relevant. Every time you teach it, spend time making it better. You are investing in your classroom experience, and you are showing pride in your work. That is what being a professional educator is all about.

Go through all the assignments you plan on giving your students. Fill out the worksheets, answer the review questions and take your own tests. See what the student sees. Part of the preparation process is not only knowing the material but also being able to understand what you are asking of your own students.

Creating the assignments and the educational materials, or at the very least, using the book resources, is just the beginning. Once you have created the material, set it aside and come back to it later. That will give you a fresh eye so you can see things you previously missed. Re-read the directions. Do they portray what you want? Look at the questions on the exams, then look at the answers. Do they make sense?

You should never ask your students to do something you have not done yourself. If you have never done it before, how will you be able to answer their questions and give directions appropriately?

Prepping takes time and energy to accomplish successfully. Your textbook will become your new best friend. Read it, learn it, and use it to the best of your ability. Try to incorporate the materials given to hit all different types of learning styles and levels of student needs. Change things up and keep it interesting. You are the captain of the ship. Chart a fun course of discovery!

Celebrate Success and Failure

> *"Success consists of going from failure to failure*
> *without loss of enthusiasm."*
> —*Winston Churchill*

How do you celebrate mistakes, and how do you celebrate success? The simple thing is to call them out and be honest about them. Everyone loves to get an award or certificate! If you screw up, acknowledge it, own it, and move on, but most importantly, learn from it. Have frank conversations like, "I did this" and "I shouldn't have done that." Those debriefs and evaluations are part of this process.

If you recorded the training, review it, and see how long it took the students to accomplish a task or to find a problem. When you watch the video in class, it brings to light how they look when performing the skill. The students will find this uncomfortable, but it is a great mirror test for themselves. Teaching involves reflection on what students know and where they need to be. The students should understand the value of practicing this skill.

The most important idea to remember is to not punish mistakes but to accept them with open arms. Embracing them shows students it is okay to screw up—that is what practice and training situations are for. Celebrate the screw-ups, make light of them if they are funny, and demonstrate that learning is a process. Some light self-deprecation adds humor to the situation. The teacher needs to exemplify the attitude mistakes happen and no one is perfect.

It is imperative you communicate to the group we can all learn from our mistakes. It is not only acceptable to make them, but important. We all learn from each other, and if we are open and honest about what we did right and what we did wrong, then we all learn from the practice and the process.

As the teacher, you set the stage; you need to come forward and say, "Okay, let's do the wrap-up, and let me start with my list of five or ten mistakes I made." Being open and willing to start sets the example. It demonstrates that mistakes happen, but we need to understand them and adapt to change for the better.

We all make mistakes, and practice and drills are the best times for this, because it prevents mistakes when the stakes are higher. Your students will see, learn, and grow from your example.

Besides admitting mistakes and accepting failures, you must explain how you plan to improve. Go through the improvement process as a group and learn together. If you lack background knowledge, show the students how to find more informational material. If it is a small technique issue, find the research and go through the tools. Whatever the weak point is, admit it and demonstrate how to improve the situation.

The goal is to make progress, improve, and avoid making those mistakes again. Through open and honest communication, you will enhance your learning environment. Be the example. Then, stand back and watch your class learn from each other.

Motivate Me!

One of the keys to success in life is motivation. Motivation can make or break a person in any endeavor they choose. This is especially true for students. How do we get motivated? Is our motivation tied to morale? Is it linked to engagement? Is it part of a communication strategy?

The simple answer is yes. Motivation includes all those aspects and more. As a teacher, it is imperative you find ways to motivate your students. Positive or negative enforcement is typically a starting point for primary motivating factors.

When I was playing football as a kid, I had great coaches, and I had some that were not so terrific. Some thought they could motivate us by telling us if we lost a game, we would have to run laps by the number of points we lost the game by. We only lost one game that year, and the score was 7-6. Thank God only one lap. But was that effective motivation? Were we motivated by the thought of punishment or suffering that kept us on the winning path?

The aspect of running laps as punishment was not part of my thinking as an athlete. I wanted to triumph because I loved winning, and I enjoyed playing with my friends and competing against those who were in battle with me. The thought of running didn't really enter our minds at all during the games. We were motivated by each other and by our success on the field.

Motivation is the drive, the internal effort you put forth to accomplish something. As a teacher, it is a tough challenge to create motivation for your students. Finding a way to do it is a key to your success.

As an emergency services instructor, you have the fortune of having a captive audience of students who are there because they chose to be there. They already have a desire to achieve something, so there is no need to convince them to take your class. Step one in motivation is done.

They came in on their own, but it is in your wheelhouse now to keep them motivated. You must find ongoing ways to keep the students active and successful participants in the course who develop their own motivation to finish strong. The type of motivation a teacher needs to demonstrate is different than other motivating factors. Simply put, you need to continue to find ways to encourage your students to successfully get to the end. So how do we achieve this?

I have found success with positive reinforcement. Try offering bonus points for exams or getting out of quizzes by achieving high scores on projects. Give rewards for putting in extra effort. This fosters a high level of learning and excellence, but it also sets a higher bar and rewards those who put in the extra effort to achieve high grades. It may even spark a competitive spirit in the room.

Another way to provide positive reinforcement is to acknowledge a student for being a group leader and mentor for others. Using students who may have higher knowledge or more experience as an example will help motivate others and show there are common and achievable skillsets. Use the resources you have in the room!

Some people are rewarded by praise and medals, certificates, or the like. Single out great acts of duty when in training on scenarios or in team skills. Handing out achievement stickers is one example.

Motivation in the classroom is better suited to using the carrot and not the stick. In my experience, I have found it is a far easier job to motivate by using excellent communication skills. Give praise and reward moral and ethical behavior rather than turning your class into a Machiavellian fear fest.

Motivating students is a huge factor for any teacher. Be positive, be focused, and be helpful. Show your students they have the power to drive themselves toward great achievements.

Use Your Time Wisely

During one parent-teacher conference, a parent started yelling at me about why I give so much homework, why I don't do my job better, and so on and so forth. The parents were upset because they said their daughter was spending too much time at home trying to get her work done for my class. I sat and patiently listened. Then I asked the student, who was with her mother, if I gave her time at the end of class to get a start on any homework.

She had to say "Yes," because it was the truth. I always gave my students time to at least start their work. I then asked the student what she chose to do instead of working on the assignment. The student didn't say much but muffled something about talking with her friends. That was the end of our conversation, and the mother apologized.

"If you don't have time to do it right,
when will you have time to do it over?"
—John Wooden

We all sometimes need to reevaluate what we spend our time on. Organization is key to helping us figure this out. Planning and preparing for your class will show you how much time you need to spend on one thing or another. Time flies, and we cannot get any more of it. Sometimes we need to ask ourselves if we are spending the time we have on the right things. Is there something else you should be focusing on? Is there other work that is more important or time-sensitive? Or is it something I can assign the students to work on themselves rather than spend time on the topic in class? When you plan always go through the work you are assigning BEFORE you assign it to the students. This is when you can gauge the time involved on it and you can adequately schedule for it. If an assignment takes you five minutes to complete then figure that it will take at least ten for your students.

I know how hard it is to get high-quality training in at a high volume. We are often pulled in so many different directions it can be very confusing and frustrating. Directives come down to do more with less. We can always be expected to accomplish extra without being given the needed time to succeed.

When it comes time to schedule hands-on work think about set-up and take-down. Be efficient with your time and be efficient in your training.

Training should focus on the skills and procedures we rarely use. Go through your curriculum and look for those areas where the highest levels of knowledge, application, and skill are used. Identify them and plan your training to increase the difficulty as the course goes on and learning increases.

Since time is short, it is important to relay to your students that their time in training is also vital. I try to convey that I will not waste their time in class with menial tasks. Rather, we get to the root and the core of the skills and abilities they will need to know and understand.

One technique for making the most of training time with emergency medical services (EMS) students is to focus on the least invasive to most invasive procedures. This means, even for those high-acuity calls, start out with the basics and work your way up into the higher-level skills. If you forget to do something simple, you will look like someone who doesn't know what they are doing. For example, as a paramedic, you should do a simple head tilt chin lift before getting ready to intubate an airway. Look for the simple answers first before you jump into pulling out every medication and needle you own. Simple fixes take the least amount of time and solve most problems.

The fire service also has a plan of action. In my department, we use the acronym SLICERS, which stands for Size-up, Locate the fire, Isolate fire flow path, Cool the fire, Extinguish, Rescue needs, and Salvage property. Yes, in the fire service, we put the cold wet stuff on top of the hot red stuff. As simple as it sounds, it is the truth.

Use the limited time you have in class to exemplify this idea. Time management is key in emergency services. Illustrate this to your students and spend your own time in preparation wisely.

Teaching Tools: Don't Reinvent the Wheel

What is a tool? Tools are supposed to help you accomplish a task. Teaching tools can be varied and diverse. They can be videos, notes, lectures, hands-on items, checklists, acronyms, or even people. These are the learning aids you will employ throughout your lesson to help facilitate the process of education.

Your toolbox will start out empty, but as time goes on and as you grow as an educator, you will end up with a giant, beautiful, red-enameled, multi-drawered toolbox on wheels; and it will take a small van to load and bring with you.

Your teaching aids will change with time and as technology evolves, but the basis for them will remain the same. They are meant to support the student's grasp of the concepts and to reach higher levels of cognitive development and learning.

One of the most helpful things you can do is compile a list of resources, including people you can contact about the subjects or material you've been asked to teach. These people can help you with subject material such as hidden secrets and shortcuts. They could be guest lecturers or proctors for your students. Sometimes people know others with the answers you seek or the experience you are looking for. When it comes right down to it, sometimes it does really make a difference in who you know. If you don't know anyone to list, the easiest thing to do is start asking around and networking with the people you meet. Go to workshops and conferences. Speak to officers or instructors from your department, from neighboring departments, or from other colleges. Ask where they got their information and what their classes are like. If they don't have answers, don't lose faith; just keep asking.

You do not need to reinvent the wheel, beg, borrow, and steal what you can. Look online and find free resources. Ask other instructors or find local businesses for help. Contact the local window or door company to see if they could donate some samples that you can use to make props. Ask the local high school or technical college if they have any students who need welding or woodworking projects. I have found that you never know the answer is no until you ask. If you are teaching EMS (emergency medical services), ask the local ER doctors who they like to listen to for their educational and continuing renewals. What journals do they read? Maybe they have other training resources that they no longer want or need. As you reach out, you will find that there are a lot of people who are willing to help. Start by asking and inquiring. You will be amazed at how quickly you can fill your toolbox.

Another basic teaching tool you should have is a file folder or jump drive. Found within should be example group projects, activities, scenarios, or sample information you can adapt for class. Find articles online or in magazines and books with interesting supplemental information. Have real-world examples and cases to show how important your subject is. Keep it relevant and keep it up-to-date. Go through those files every couple of years to make sure that they are still the best standard available. We all learn more when we see how important it can be in real life-and-death circumstances.

Important note: if you do use articles, online material, or recordings, make sure you give proper credence to their authors. Ensure you are using your proper copyright and permissions for any materials. Free and fair use is one thing but give credit where credit is due and show your students how the process works!

The website I developed for this book (www.twodarkthirty.com) has a plethora of resources and sample lesson plans you can use to make your own. My advice for emergency services is to use the tools you would in a real-life situation or in a department. If you are teaching cardiology, then use the monitor you have access to. Do a 12-lead ECG, and have your students read through many examples. Think about the steps involved in the entire process of doing a 12-lead ECG. Make a checklist for it while you are at it and put it in your toolbox.

Likewise, if you are doing high-rise deployment, then put your turn-out gear on and make a high-rise pack, run the hose tower, and connect the standpipes. If you are talking about ropes and knots, then do what my dad did when I was a kid and have your students tie knots with their fire gloves on under a table. My dad told me, "Marc, when you're in a fire you can't see, and you'll have your gloves on too!" Make it realistic.

If you are training on drug searches in a vehicle, then use a real car and bring in a search dog to help make it realistic. Use the tools of the trade. The more your students are familiar with what they will use daily, the better they can prepare for and execute their jobs at Two Dark Thirty. Remember, education is more than just learning; it is using knowledge, applying it to real situations, and solving problems. This is the path to true wisdom.

Mr. Hill's Notes:

- Clearly communicate the rules.

- Manage your classroom effectively with flexibility and firmness.

- Empathy and compassion have their place.

- Be prepared for class.

- Don't reinvent the wheel. Start filling your toolbox.

- Celebrate the successes and the failures.

- Keep motivating students' success.

- Learn from your mistakes.

Search and entry training 2007. Member at door is 19 years old, middle member is 36 years old, and rear member is 52 years old. All ages at the time of the photo. Your audience can drastically change and very. (Photo courtesy of the author)

Chapter Four

WHO ARE YOUR STUDENTS?

"A good teacher, like a good entertainer, first must hold the audience's attention, then they can teach the lesson."
—*John Henrik Clarke*

I walked to school when I was your age, and it was uphill in both directions!

This classic phrase tells the tale of the woe and misery of the prior generations. As a parent, I've caught myself telling this same old tale to my daughters about having to do something that was immensely hard with no help at all. It is useful at the moment, especially with the younger ones who usually roll their eyes after hearing it. The point of the story is supposed to show you have done something far worse than what you are asking them to do--so shut up and take the grief! The phrase also usually implies you should not question the directions given to you.

In the fire service, I often hear tales of how easy we have it now versus when the veterans started. They would often tell stories of old chiefs saying if you don't like something, then get out because there are five hundred others just waiting in line for your job. Or how they used to line up for inspection at the beginning of each shift with their dress blues (Class A uniforms) on.

That has changed today. We often have trouble finding qualified candidates to fill entry-level firefighter and paramedic positions. It is not like it used to be. Circumstances have changed.

Growing up in a small mining town in Michigan's Upper Peninsula, my dad was on the local volunteer fire department. He would often take me and my sisters down to the "fire hall" to roll up the hose and wash the fire trucks. We grew up having our birthday parties in the fire hall kitchen and dining room. We were allowed to ride on the fire trucks in parades and threw candy at other kids.

There was a tradition, and the local community supported the fire department. Over the past three decades, in the USA, there has been a doubling of the training and time required to volunteer. Most families today have both parents working and there is less availability to volunteer and children are less exposed to the service. We need to acknowledge this change and plan for how we will accomplish our mission in this new environment.

What we can do as educators is find ways to reach more of our audience, our students. If we can spread the word about the value of service and of a career in giving back to our communities then I think we may have a chance at real positive change. In order to do that successfully, it will take all of the emergency services to push that positive message and open the minds of our communities. To push a message we need to first understand who we are talking to.

Our Students are our Audience

Understanding where someone has come from or their life experiences are paramount in education. Keeping your students engaged and focused on their learning is a big part of teaching. It is amazing how differently time has changed.

I was born in 1980, so I am part of the transitional generation, rather than a Millennial or a Generation X'er. I have attributes from both generations.

I grew up in the eighties when we didn't have cable television, only local public channels. There was no Internet. Computers were expensive, and all were located at school. The computer screens were shades of green. Some of the more affluent kids had Atari or Nintendo.

Our parents expected us to be outside riding our bikes, getting lost in the neighborhood, and not hanging around inside our homes. We were supposed to be seen and not heard. For the most part, we played by ourselves or with our friends, and my parents barely knew where I was most of the time. Supper was at six o'clock, and in my hometown of Negaunee, Michigan, they would ring a siren in the summer, alerting the kids to the time. You had better be home to eat, or you had no food, or it was ice cold.

I grew up on the cusp of change between generations. I remember being taught how to use a computer as a tool, but I learned how to type on a typewriter. We had basic computer games like Oregon Trail, and by Middle School, we started to have dial-up internet available on only one computer in the library, for which you had to sign up for fifteen-minute sessions. I remember America Online (AOL) and Prodigy online databases. Cell phones were in giant bags and were only for extreme emergencies because they were so expensive. Fast food was eaten when we went somewhere for special occasions. We used our imaginations to create spaceships and time machines out of refrigerator boxes, and we actually played with our toys.

There are multiple generations in the workforce, but as an example, let's focus on one. Nowadays, the youth are referred to as Generation Y or Generation Z. This group seems to get the most flack, so I will use them as the example generation. These individuals barely remember the events of September 11th, 2001. They've never known a time without a computer that didn't have direct high-speed internet access. They don't remember a time without a cell phone or smartphone, and they don't remember a time without social media. They have always been able to instantly get information by asking Alexa, Siri, or Google. Their entire lives have been spent online and plugged in, and their parents have published their lives by posting pictures online for all to see.

According to the Centers for Disease Control (CDC), over 50% of this combined generation group, Y and Z, have grown up in single-parent homes. Many of them have parents or guardians who worked or were busy most of the time. Sometimes these are referred to as 'latch-key kids' because they were expected to come home by themselves.

This generation has fast food or ready-to-eat meals on a regular basis. Their interactions with people are diminished, especially when you calculate the time they spend online (the CDC found that between the ages of 8 and 18, children spend an average of 7.5 hours a day in front of a screen). They are more comfortable texting than calling and speaking. That being said, they often work well on their own and have a terrific grasp of technology. They understand the potential of the internet and know how to use, apply, and coordinate with it, such as through social media.

In the workforce today, we have many different generations (gens) working together. They include the remaining Baby Boomers, Gen Xers, Millennials, Gen Y, and Z. They all have their history and their upbringing to make them who they are, as well as the different lives they lead.

As teachers and leaders, we should strive to reach all of them. Our businesses and our classrooms are filled with them, and we should make an effort to understand who they are, what they represent, and how to interact with and reach them. You will be amazed at how this practice will enhance your classroom experience for both the instructor and the students.

Socioeconomic Status

A concept teachers must deal with and understand is socioeconomic status (SES). This is how much money people make or earn a year, combined with their education, family structure, and employment status. It can also be the social status or group people identify with. These groups are commonly identified as the rich, poor, middle-class, white-collar, blue-collar, and so forth.

Humanity comes from many different backgrounds and many different family structures. Many people were raised in households where parents were divorced, with a single mother or a single father, and some lived with foster families. We were all raised in different households, in different ways, and we have all had to deal with difficulties and life's challenges.

Those differences in how we are raised are also things educators must understand and acknowledge in their students. What a student identifies as normal behavior is strongly rooted in their upbringing.

The amount of money a family has access to will directly affect the way a person grows up. Whether both parents work or are together, and the types of careers and education a parent chooses, will influence the child's 'norms'. The yearly family income will link them to a home or neighborhood. This may, in turn, relate to the success of the schools they attend. The public schools directly relate to the quality of education and the number of opportunities the students have available to them. Available activities will contribute to their overall development of team building, rapport, drive, and motivation to succeed. Family income also correlates with the expectations of where or what the child does after school, such as college or direct skilled labor.

Growing up with severe challenges like where your next meal comes from or whether the heat or water has been shut off could drastically change a person's outlook on life. Immediate problems need to be addressed daily, often limiting a long-term perspective. The economic level will also drastically change how a person perceives the structure of government services, and their trust or lack thereof. They could accept authority or run from it in fear.

We must understand that we all come from different walks of life and different circumstances. A good educator will know, or at the very least try, to understand their students. Be aware of the situation and circumstances of your students. This will help you with your classroom management style and with planning the direction of your course.

Economic Class Characteristics

Within the class structure of society, there are oftentimes varying degrees of relevance and importance to certain aspects of the lives of the students. Philip Devol authored a book in 2020 entitled, *'Getting Ahead in a just-getting-by World.'* He argues the generational cycle of poverty and lower SES is rooted in a cyclical class struggle. This struggle creates a seemingly never-ending process. The drive for monetary freedom and to get ahead causes strife. People are asked to give up personal time for working longer or harder hours. The struggle is found when the clash between the two is seen and felt. Devol saw that personal friendships and family tend to be the most important aspects of the lives of people with lower SES. They prioritize the significance of those relationships over any educational needs they may have. This in turn limits their abilities to get out of their class struggle causing them to stay where they are.

These students will have issues and difficulty with assignments when they are forced to choose between getting their work done and helping a friend or family member. As the instructor, you will need to deal with this and create a clear message, with flexibility and firmness. You understand the relevant issues with empathy and compassion, but their education needs have to find a place in their priorities.

I frequently hear many justifications as to why a student has not finished an assignment or project. The typical 'dog ate my homework' excuse is a result of a family member in trouble, a lack of computer time, or other job/health-related issues or emergencies. Be empathetic to their plight and hear them. However, there needs to be a set standard and a level of expectation.

It is imperative that within the first week of class you have a conversation about planning and time management with the students. Have the students create a plan-for-success guide for themselves. Go through the syllabus and clearly state when items are due and how the assignments must be accomplished. Review the entire process with them. Show them it is possible to have their family lives and hobbies along with being a successful student. The choice is theirs. Be open to their issues but resolve to have knowledge and understanding of how SES might affect their education.

According to Devol (5), those in the middle to higher SES classes tend to sacrifice their family and friends for their education. These groups will limit their time with outside distractions and focus on their work. Their family circumstances have shown them education equals higher pay and higher prestige. They have seen that hard work pays off. Their family members have also seen this, and they will not question them for choosing schoolwork over a family need. This class accepts the challenges that education gives them. However, this group also tends to have limited social skills and needs to work harder to develop those relationships. They will get their work done, but at a cost to a team mentality because their goal is to complete the work—even if they think they must do it themselves, all alone.

Classes of SES and how they will affect your students are important to understand. Your students will be a diverse group that comes from many walks of life. As a teacher, it is important for you to understand your audience and how they will interact with each other. Take the time before class to research who your students are and where you can take the class. Sometimes this information is available prior to class. If it is not then spend some valuable time on the first day of the class talking to your students. Or speak to them individually during some work time. Make the effort. Knowing your audience's background will help you be a successful instructor.

Generational Interaction...Making it Happen!

"Education is simply the soul of a society as it passes from one generation to another."
—*Gilbert K. Chesterton*

So, the million-dollar question is, how do you get all these generational and societal differences to work together successfully?

I have seen some volunteer fire and EMS departments that have grandfathers, grandmothers, grandsons, granddaughters, nieces, nephews, friends, and family—all groups of people, multiple generations, interacting and working together as a successful team.

In my career department, we have members who have over 30 years of experience and others who have just literally started their careers and have never driven an ambulance, let alone a multi-ton fire engine. How do you get those two groups to talk to each other, relate to each other, and work together successfully?

Common ground is the answer. Finding the connection that will enable the conversation to start. Getting your students to talk to each other and share their experiences will help set the environment for discussion. If they are quiet and do not want to share, then it is up to you to start the dialogue. Either way, finding common ground is important. Think about why they are there in the first place: to serve their community and to help those in need. Start off by talking about those types of concepts. The rest will follow.

Make the time to get those groups together and interact. The first day of class is a great time to talk and share stories. As the teacher, you must lead the discussion. Illustrate to the group what you would like them to find out about themselves. I have found the best way to get people to talk in any situation is by having an excuse to eat. Who doesn't love food? Who doesn't love a good barbecue? Bring in a treat for the first day of class. It could be something as simple as doughnuts or cookies. When you get everyone together to share in the food experience, they tend to talk to each other and start to understand and develop camaraderie and rapport. They will inevitably start to share stories and experiences.

It may take some effort on your part to get the party and conversations started. You may have to play game-show-host and start the interaction, but like dominoes, once they begin to fall, they will keep tumbling. As the teacher, I have found the most success by spending time on the first day of class getting to know your students and letting them get to know you. Tell a story about your own reason for being there and why you wanted to teach.

Find something all the generations in the room have in common, and find the connection between the students. In Wisconsin, it's the Green Bay Packers. Either you love them, or you hate them, but either way, you have some common ground to work off. Find out what that might be and use it to worm your way into a discussion or to get the groups to join forces together. Find common ground on which everyone can stand and build the house of communication and interaction on that solid foundation. You will be impressed with how much all the groups will have in common versus how much they do not.

As the teacher in the course, it is up to you to create the atmosphere and communication channels for your students. Understand your audience and where they came from, as well as what they may face in their upbringing. The teacher always sets the tone and example. Take the first fifteen minutes to talk to them and relate to them. Let them know you are all here for the same reason—to grow and learn together!

Use Your Students to Achieve Success

"Some are born great, some achieve greatness,
and some have greatness thrust upon them."
—William Shakespeare

Every generation has a great deal of knowledge to share. This knowledge can be social and institutional. Course instructors are not the ultimate subject experts. As I have said before if we need to find outside resources to help us aid in our instruction, do so. No one knows everything. You will find that many students in our courses have a great deal of information and experience. Don't ignore it, but finds ways to use it within our instruction.

I have found, no matter the generation, if you ask for help people respond and look to assist in any way they can. Getting multiple groups or generations to work together and contribute can be a challenge for any teacher, no matter their years of experience. This is why it is so imperative to start a group discussion on the first day of class. Finding out how much knowledge people have at the beginning will help you to identify those that might be able to help you as a teacher.

You should understand the experience, training, and time your students have spent in this profession or others. Learn from them, ask them questions, and if they respond with a curmudgeon's scornful attitude, leave them alone. Don't poke the bear. Not everyone wants to be a teacher's assistant.

Find those students later and have a private conversation with them. Compliment your target. Tell them, "Hey, with all your experience, can you please help me understand this?" or "Can you please show me how you like to run this pump?" or "Can you please walk me through how you were taught?" A little encouragement goes a long way. Let them know that you value them and that you are going to look to them to help you. I have found great success in simply asking for help in an inviting manner.

Everyone loves a compliment, and emergency services are no exception, whether they will admit it or not. Knowing that can help defuse a lot of tough and awkward situations. Compliments are always helpful, especially if they come with sincerity and honesty.

I have certainly worked with a few obstinate and annoyed people, but they were absolutely fantastic at their jobs. If you pay them a little attention, and you give them a flattering remark you are sincere about, you may see their shields drop. These types of people became some of the best assistant teachers I ever had.

Compliments are very disarming. If you give someone the time to show them you care and you want their attention, it goes a long way. It also develops a real rapport between you.

Having trust and rapport in emergency situations is vital. Veterans will know they can trust other students because they were the ones who showed the students what to do. Seeing other students succeed in stressful situations also gives students credibility and respect, because they can be trusted to act in the right manner in future events. The student-mentor scenario also gives veterans that teaching spirit, and it opens them up to new ideas. This can change the entire dynamic of your class.

The key is to find ways in which generations can complement each other. Once you find the shared vision, goal, and how they can help themselves, they will work together. Whether those are leadership-driven activities or icebreakers with team-building activities, activities like trust falls have their point. Most people can't stand them, but at the same time, there's a method to the madness. Students may not want to do an icebreaker and start by talking about one of their hobbies, but the end will justify the means. Once the talking, the rapport, and the camaraderie starts, respect is earned, and that respect leads to professionalism and trust. Let the classroom leader get the ball rolling!

As a teacher, you will help guide and push your students to know what to do in those critical moments. If you understand where some of your students and workers are coming from, you can also facilitate structural interaction. This is true whether you are in a small-town volunteer department made up of the residents such as farmers, hard workers in an industry, or home businesses owners, or if you are coming from a full-time career department where most of the applicants come straight out of school and have never worked another job outside of the fire service. Understanding someone in your charge is imperative to success. You should develop the ability to understand how both generational and socioeconomic differences affect how people see the world and interact with it.

Having your students help you will also be key when you are not in your home area. As an instructor, I usually do not have all the necessary items with me. I must come into the department or location I am teaching with only my laptop and a projector and maybe some limited supplies.

You should call ahead and speak with the administration where you may be located. Ask them if it would be alright if you used their tools and equipment. I have never had someone tell me no, but that doesn't mean that it won't happen. In the planning and prepping stage, call ahead and organize the tools you need to successfully accomplish your goals. You may find out then who is in your class and who may be willing to help you with the materials and possible teaching.

For example, if you are working with firefighters doing search and rescue scenarios, see if you can find a smoke machine to use and create a realistic environment. Get a 180-pound dummy to drag and find for search and rescue or firefighter extractions. If you are doing vehicle extrication, call a local salvage company and see if they will donate a car for you to chop up. There may be members of the organization that have more experience than you do in either training evolution. Use them, involve them, and bring them to be positive members of your team.

Use the tools you have access to, people especially. Demonstrate using your resource materials and books, but also know there is more than one way to do everything. Your way does not have to be the only right way. Perspective is important. Use your students' experiences to your advantage. Use your students to make your teaching more engaging and more memorable.

Generational Differences

"There is a mysterious cycle in human events. To some generations, much is given. Of other generations, much is expected. "
—*President Franklin D. Roosevelt*

There are many aspects of how different people are raised that every educator should know and understand. The generational changes that have happened can be quite impressive.

My grandfather was born in 1917. He grew up in a logging camp in the heart of the wild in Michigan's Upper Peninsula. He didn't see an automobile until he was twelve. The logging camp had no running water, no plumbing, and no electricity. Horses were used daily for all the work and travel. Within his lifetime, he saw airplanes go from canvas, wood, and bicycle parts to watching the moon landing by NASA in 1969. He saw written letters replaced by telegraph messages then with a household phone line. Travel shifted from trains and ships to cross-country airplane trips. All of this was accomplished within his lifetime.

Growing up when and where I did has everything to do with my attitude, beliefs, and ethics. The tough-love style was common. This approach is also how I learned to swim as a kid. My dad threw me into the deep end of the water in an abandoned mine pit, and all I remember him saying was, "You better start paddling, you better start kicking!"

I came from a generation that can handle this kind of drastic change and forcible movement. Other generations may not adjust so quickly. They have not been raised in a time when they were forced to adapt to fast-changing circumstances. A lot of students today have been constantly told how important and unique they are, how they can do anything and achieve anything in the world. They are given participation medals and trophies for just showing up. In school, some may have had poor teachers who caved to confrontation and just gave out answers rather than truly making the students learn and challenge themselves.

Just think about all the generational changes that have happened. Like my own grandfather saw, imagine what level of technological advancement will occur in your lifetime! How the world changes from youth to adulthood! Think of all the experience and knowledge people have with them. Use that knowledge and use that wisdom.

Below is an abbreviated list of generation names, titles, aspects, and information that can be very useful to you.

One size doesn't fit all when it comes to today's population—learn how to adjust to a multigenerational workforce and students we will see. (6) (7)

Baby Boomers Born 1946–1964

- Optimistic, competitive, workaholic, team-oriented.

- Shaped by: The Vietnam War, civil rights movement, Watergate.

- Motivated by: Company loyalty, teamwork, and duty.

- Communication style: Whatever is most efficient, including phone calls and face-to-face.

- Worldview: Achievement comes after paying one's dues; sacrifice for success.

- Employers should: Provide them with specific goals and deadlines; put them in mentor roles; offer coaching-style feedback.

Generation X: Born 1965–1980

- Flexible, informal, skeptical, independent.

- Shaped by: The AIDs epidemic, the fall of the Berlin Wall, and the dot-com boom.

- Motivated by: Diversity, work-life balance, their personal-professional interests rather than the company's interests.

- Communication style: Whatever is most efficient, including phone calls and face-to-face.

- Worldview: Favoring diversity; quick to move on if their employer fails to meet their needs; resistant to change at work if it affects their personal lives.

- Employers should: Give them immediate feedback; provide flexible work arrangements and work-life balance; extend opportunities for personal development.

Millennials: Born 1981–2000

- Competitive, civic-minded, open-minded on diversity, achievement-oriented

- Shaped by: Columbine, 9/11, the internet.

- Motivated by: Responsibility, the quality of their manager, unique work experiences

- Communication style: IMs, texts, and email.

- Worldview: Seeking challenge, growth, and development; fun work life and work-life balance; likely to leave an organization if they don't like change.

- Employers should: Get to know them personally; manage by results; be flexible on their schedule and work assignments; provide immediate feedback.

Generation Z: Born 2001–2020

- Global, entrepreneurial, progressive, less focused.

- Shaped by: Life after 9/11, the Great Recession, and access to technology from a young age.

- Motivated by: Diversity, personalization, individuality, and creativity.

- Communication style: IMs, texts, social media.

- Worldview: Self-identifying as digital device addicts; valuing independence and individuality; preferring to work with millennial managers, innovative coworkers, and new technologies.

- Employers should: Offer opportunities to work on multiple

projects at the same time; provide work-life balance; allow them to be self-directed and independent.

Mr. Hill's Notes:

- Know who your audience is and get to know them.

- Start by talking.

- Find common ground among students.

- Use the experience in the classroom to help you.

- Yes, there are many generational distinctions… and it is okay.

- All generations have something to share and contribute.

Haz-mat Technician Training Situational Awareness dummy 2021. While doing entries and identification for hazardous chemical spills the instructors wanted to make a point that you should always be aware of the call incident and surroundings. This was the "caller" of the spill at a local pool where unknown chemical "Chlorine" was leaking. Caller was a bomber looking to attack first responders. (Photo courtesy of author)

Chapter Five

How to Educate in Emergency Services

"Far and away the best prize that life offers is the chance to work hard at work worth doing."
—President Theodore Roosevelt

E arly in the morning, Station 3, Ambulance 3, were dispatched to a home where a woman was in active labor, and she was only twenty-eight weeks pregnant. We heard this radio dispatch at Station 1 and started to roll our ambulance toward the address just in case there were issues.

Most of the time, when we get these kinds of calls, there is no baby on the way, but there can be other issues that may seem like active labor. We were hoping for the latter. However, after a short two minutes of driving toward the call, the lead paramedic on scene requested our help with Code 3 (EMERGENCY) RIGHT NOW! We hit the lights and sirens and raced to the home address.

When we arrived, we rushed in with all our tools and bags in hand. I walked into the bathroom, looked down, and saw the expectant mother on her back in the middle of the bathroom floor. The baby was not quite out of the mother at this point. My fellow firefighter/paramedic was holding the baby's tiny, bluish legs in his hands. I knew immediately not only was this a REAL emergency, but this was also a full-breech birth (feet first, not headfirst as is normal), and ten weeks premature. Despite all our training, fear and tension were thick in the room. On top of it all, we learned she had lost her prior two pregnancies.

It felt like forever standing in the doorway, but only split seconds passed. As I looked down at my coworker and he looked up at me, his pale face and wide eyes showed me he was screaming on the inside, and I didn't blame him. The baby's legs were blue, meaning there was an oxygen deficiency. Most likely, the cord was wrapped around the baby's neck, suffocating his supply of fresh oxygenated blood. I knelt next to him and started to help. There was some time to work with, but we needed to deliver this baby fast. We worked together to move the baby's legs and make enough room for the baby to come out with the mother's next contraction. We told her to push. She did, and carefully we pulled out the little infant. It was a boy! We worked quickly to cut the umbilical cord. I took the tiny baby in my hand (he fit nearly perfectly with his small size) and went to our waiting stretcher outside the bathroom.

The baby was extremely small and needed our help. I knew from his color he needed oxygen, and I knew we needed to actively get him to breathe on his own. We tried to rub him to stimulate him, but he was still very limp and not making any sounds. I took the suction device and attempted to suction out his little nose and mouth the best I could. We needed venous access, so my partner drilled an intraosseous (bone) needle into his leg to help get fluids into the baby.

His heart rate was also slow. I placed the cardioversion pads on the baby, but he was so tiny I had to place one on his front and one on his back. We gave him a drug called Epinephrine to try to increase his heart rate, and, at the same time, I attempted to suction more fluid and mucus out of his mouth. I knew he was far too small for any of our pediatric intubation tools. We connected our monitor, and I started to give slow, small breaths with Oxygen as my partner did manual compressions on the baby's chest to try to both stimulate and increase his heart rate. I looked at the monitor—we had a carbon dioxide (CO_2) exchange reading. This was a huge sign. It meant the baby was breathing on his own with our help. The heart rate was increasing, and we decided to give him a little more Epinephrine and transport him immediately.

Ambulance 3's crew drove lights and sirens to the hospital with the baby. My partner and I waited for the mother to deliver her placenta and then loaded her into our ambulance and took her and her husband to the hospital. We decided to go emergency (lights and sirens) as well. We didn't know if the baby was going to continue to improve or if we needed to get his new mother and father to the ER to say goodbye. We blasted our way through the city and arrived in the ER to find the baby had been taken in an isolette to the NICU (Neonatal Intensive Care Unit) of the hospital. To our relief, the doctors congratulated us. They were all amazed and impressed by what we had done. One of the doctors said, "One in a million chances, and you made it. I don't know if I could even have done what you did on the floor of a bathroom without all my staff and equipment."

"Luck is where opportunity meets preparation."
—Seneca

As much as it was a stressful and hard situation, his words meant a lot to us. It took me days to really process what we had done. All of us who were a part of the call received our fire department's Core Values Award. The recognition was nice, but the best thing was being invited by the parents to come and see the baby about a month later. Seeing him breathe on his own and seeing that he had grown bigger than he was in my hands a month before was enough reward.

This story demonstrates even in the most stressful and emergent situations, time and care can be taken to slow everything down, get back to your training, and complete the task at hand. You can find places to teach all the time. I knew the fear and dread I saw in my coworker's eyes during that situation. We all felt that way. It was a true emergency. Delivering a baby is one of the rare events in EMS but delivering a breech baby is even rarer. My coworker was doing a great job showing confidence and demonstrating his calmness, but I knew what he was feeling on the inside because I was feeling the same thing: outright panic. Our training kicked in, and we all worked together as a team to achieve success. None of us could have done it alone. We triumphed together.

In that moment, we barely talked about what we were doing; we were in the groove, and we all knew what needed to be done. This is the best outcome of critical stress training. We had practiced and had gone through scenarios before, but this time it was for real, and we needed to be on our A-game. The lives of the baby and the mother were at stake and literally in our hands. Thankfully, perhaps with help from above, we did it and everything worked out. It makes my list of true miracles I have witnessed and been a part of.

Training and teaching, even at this moment, was possible. I knelt next to my coworker and encouraged him through the birthing process. This enabled us to both bring about a successful outcome. I knew, from having had the experience of helping deliver all three of my own daughters, what to do and how to do it. We worked together, and I helped teach even at this most important moment. There are always teachable moments, and there is always time to demonstrate or talk someone through an imperative procedure. The adage of learning something new every day is appropriate. You can always find the time to learn, no matter what is going on or what the day brings.

Field Training

One of the best ways to learn a foreign language is by throwing yourself into the situation and culture. The immersive environment forces you to change your thinking, to listen, and process the new language. It is challenging, but after a few weeks, you really start to improve. Being forced to live in a new language gives you no choice but to learn and adapt. Some of the best training happens when you are actually doing the job you intend to do.

Field training is more of a one-on-one situation than a large class-room atmosphere. This type of training deals directly with a single student, or at the very least, a small few. The preceptor, or field training officer (FTO), should have a game plan drawn up with their direct supervisors. Clinical hours and time spent acting in the role of the position are examples of this type of education. Training in this environment is personal. It deals directly with content knowledge, job skills, KSA, and expectations.

The FTO, as a trainer, is also a teacher and should accept that responsibility. Field training is often the last part of a student's or new employee's orientation or final work. This can make or break them. It is imperative, if you are the FTO, you use direct and higher-order thinking skills to assess the student. Make them demonstrate complex procedures or actions. Have them explain the reasoning behind certain medications. Give them the opportunity to explain fire flow path or ventilation strategies. I have found the most success in talking through or doing walkthroughs of situations.

By the time they have become part of field training or clinical review hours, students should have had all their core content knowledge and coursework (didactic) completed. They should be familiar with the job skills and expectations of the position. If they are not familiar, make sure you communicate with them on day one. The first part of any successful field training is being aware of the rules and the procedures for the work to be accomplished.

One of the hardest parts of being in this position as an FTO is letting go and allowing the student to work. It may take the student some time to evaluate the situation, but you need to have patience. It is hard to do, especially when seconds count. Giving them an extra five seconds will seem like forever, but it will allow them to process the situation and make decisions. Step back and be patient.

Field training should be done with members that are familiar with the concepts of teaching and are open to having the students with them. Assigning the student to a group that is not open to this type of training will trouble the ones being voluntold (voluntarily told) to do it, and this will come across in their attitudes and their demeanor. Save your students the hassle of a bad or failing experience and assign them to a unit or members who are open to the type of work needed for a successful experience. This is one of the biggest reasons I wrote this book. I want to help those who are found in this kind of position. It is extremely hard to find yourself in a situation where you have no experience, education, or training. I've seen many FTOs who have been told to "figure it out." So do your students a favor and find the FTO who has the willingness to learn or has the right attitude to teach.

On-the-job (OTJ) training is common in a lot of career fields. Emergency services are no exception. There are many pearls of wisdom and knowledge you can learn by doing your job. Tricks of the trade, hints, shortcuts, and other useful knowledge is passed down from one crew to another.

However, the aspect of not knowing and the need to continue learning must be understood by all. When someone new starts, no matter how, where, or when they come in, they need to be given the freedom to learn and grow within the group. High expectations are one thing, but unrealistic expectations are another. OTJ training is a great way to evaluate past learning and knowledge. It shows the instructor or trainer where the gaps in knowledge are, what you can skip, and how to spend your time in the most value-added way. As a teacher, the OTJ training can be used for helping groups work together and to find the best leaders for the different activities or evolutions. OTJ training also shows the instructor where their students can best fit into a group.

Set your students, staff, and yourself up for success by having a written plan of attack, understandable expectations, and policies for doing any type of field training. All parties should acknowledge the challenges before them and should accept them. Empower your students by giving them the responsibility to act on the skills they have been trained to do. Give them the freedom to make mistakes and to learn from them. Starting off on the right foot will ensure that the training is achieved in a positive way and will be followed by a long-lasting career.

The Dunning-Kruger Effect

Figure 2: Confidence vs. Competence Chart based on Trainingpeaks.com

"They have no idea what they don't know."

This is a line my former battalion chief used to say. This expression is related to a psychological study and the bias of a person who is basically unaware of how little they understand about a given situation. They have limited knowledge, but what they do know and understand makes them aware enough to be dangerous--they know enough to think they know it all.

In emergency services, we often see these types of individuals as the 'three-year veteran'. They have been on the job just long enough to think they know it all and have seen it all. Those actual veterans, who have far more experience and wisdom, know they just don't get it yet. As the chart describes we see that we all start off fresh with all kinds of information and new thinking. We know it all. We are brimming with optimism and enthusiasm.

As a teacher, it will be hard to challenge these types of folks. They will often give you an attitude and have an aura of overconfidence. Many people demonstrate this type of bravado and a "salty" arrogance because they think they have seen it all. In reality, the limited experience they have may cause them to be dangerous for the crew and for themselves. They will risk a lot to save a little. They will not have the situational awareness to know what dangerous signs to look for and what to expect if they see something happening.

This is where you come in. It is imperative, as the instructor, you point out the pitfalls and the risks associated with the challenges. Within your lesson, state the obvious and discuss the possibilities. Point out the situations that might happen, given a cause-and-effect relationship. Find articles and true-life stories to share. Bring in speakers or find other experts to augment your methods.

The lack of real-world knowledge and experience will be evident. Gauge your students and find out what they know and what they think they understand. The Dunning-Kruger effect (see figure 2 (8)) shows the direct path a normal person will take on their journey through experience and years of service.

We all reach a point where we think we have competence, only to come up against a brick wall that shows us we have no idea. This saps our spirit and our confidence. We doubt ourselves and our abilities. Eventually, we continue and grow to the point of acceptance. We gain enough real-world experience to understand our own limitations and shortcomings and rebuild our confidence. This is only achieved through hard work and years of service.

Eventually, we get to where we need to be. Not an expert but highly competent and confident. But as instructors, we need to understand what our students may be thinking and believing. Remember, getting all our students to the finish line is the goal. Education is a journey that takes time. Illustrate that belief and challenge your students to grow past what they believe they "think" they know.

Graham's Core Tasks

Figure 3: Risk/Frequency Chart. Based on Gordon Graham at Lex ipol.com

Gordon Graham is a retired California Highway Patrol (CHP) officer, lawyer, author, and speaker. He has further divided the classic risk-frequency chart. Within the four-square (see figure 3) areas, Gordon has concentrated on emergency calls within the high-risk (HR) and low-frequency (LF) areas in the top left. He speaks to the calls within this area as either no discretionary time (NDT) or discretionary time (DT) (9). The NDT calls are the ones that require "core critical tasks" the kinds of tasks and skills that Gordon says are "very risky, done very rarely, with no time to think." These critical tasks, within the NDT calls, are the ones we need to spend time training and focusing on. Take the time to identify and develop those tasks. Find out what skills are needed to react and perform with no time to think. The core skills of the NDT abilities.

If we think about the types of calls an average emergency services department might have, the majority of the calls are found in the lower right corner. The low-risk, and high-frequency (LR/HF) section. The mundane and routine calls we handle with little to no thought.

Mr. Graham argues we should never waste our time training on LR/HF calls. He argues that the HR/LF calls that are discretionary time (DT) give us some wiggle room to act. These calls are serious, but we have the time to step back and analyze them. However not realizing this and not using the time to identify the situation will cause harm.

Gordon argues for spending your training and education on those NDT events with the use of critical tasks. These are the calls we rarely see and really require a lot of resources, manpower, and equipment. These calls also have substantial life-or-death risks. When these calls happen, we need to react and act immediately. We have no time to think.

All we need to do is look at the line-of-duty deaths (LODD) that occur every year. These incident reports are full of situations and occurrences that put lives at risk. Reading through these and looking at the close calls or near misses will give you a glimpse as to what types of training in critical tasks you could be and really should be doing.

As a teacher, look at the curriculum and see where you can spend more time training for those NDT HR/LF events. Do not waste time on things that are not detrimental or life-threatening. Time is precious. We rarely have time to do what we really want to accomplish. Do you really want to live with the fact you spent sixty minutes on routine behavior, or do you want to train on life-saving techniques and those critical skills that can and will save lives?

Spend your time training for an event that, God willing, will never occur. Train for the types of events that only happen once every decade. Focusing on those types of events and scenarios provides for proper training and education. It shows that you have the student's best interest at heart.

Communicate this importance to your students. They will acknowledge you are making the correct decisions about what to train the on, and you will earn respect for those decisions. You will earn respect for having taught the course with enthusiasm and purpose.

Take the time to plan out valuable training and educational opportunities. Don't just watch YouTube videos. Get out in the field and run through critical scenarios. Walk through possibilities and run backup plans and contingency plans that could happen during these high-risk, low-frequency events.

As the instructor, take those no discretionary time (NDT) events and turn them into key training. Spend the needed training time for events that could kill a person. It also enables you to train and use time wisely, so you have multiple processes going on all at the same time.

When it comes right down to it, in the real world, we must perform our job duties during multiple events that are happening at the same time. Usually, we are being hit in multiple directions with multiple arrows, and you're just trying to dart, dive, duck, and dodge to the best of your ability. As the instructor, spend your prep time researching where you can best fit this type of high-risk and low-frequency training into your schedule. Concentrate on those core critical tasks. Make room for it!

Implementing High-Risk Scenarios

These types of training events involve a great deal of coordination and planning. Because of this high-risk scenarios usually are only done on a quarterly or less basis. When dealing with any kind of scenario-based training, it is very important to do a walkthrough and talk about the plan of action. As an instructor, organize the plan and have everything written down. The training incident should be written down and include the following features:

1. *Training topic and/or brief description.*

2. *Training date and time of event and brief schedule of the events of the day.*

3. *Location, place, and/or address of training.*

4. *Instructor names along with any adjuncts and/or advisers.*

5. *Is this an ISO (Insurance Services Office Inc.) or EMS qualifying refresher training? This is a yes or no question.*

6. *Objectives (at least three) of the training.*

7. *Key concepts* (at least three) *or teaching points of influence.*

8. *Emergency information and all danger or hazard concerns.*

9. *Suggested drill adaptions or variations based on training level. This could be ways to make it harder or easier for your students.*

You should have examples of materials printed out. like maps or street diagrams. Students need to know what the operation will entail and what roles they will be playing. This does not mean revealing all the training possibilities. Some things need to be kept secret so you can see their reactions, but overall, the big picture should be understood. Goals, missions, and some structural characteristics need explanation. The event should be walked through from a certain standpoint, and everyone should know what they may or may not be graded on, or what their purpose and role will be.

> *"No man is worth his salt who is not ready at all times*
> *to risk his well-being, to risk his body, to risk his life, in*
> *a great cause."*
> —*President Theodore Roosevelt*

The main details of the scenario are there, but there will be obstacles the students will have to overcome. Some people may have to play victims, while others may be bystanders that get in your way. Other challenges include elements such as a group of bystanders, barking dogs, dead hydrants, prolonged power company or gas company shutoffs, or possible criminal behavior at the scene. Reactions to these obstacles will be seen, and the adaptations that are made should be documented.

Here are some examples of this type of training you may want to incorporate:

- *RIT Firefighter trapped with physical barrier removal.*

- *Multi-victim search and rescue.*

- *Choking, cardiac arrest/pulseless non-breather (PNB) of infant.*

- *Surgical cricothyrotomy airway.*

- *Stab/gun wound packing(s).*

- *Impinged victim in auto extrication with compartment syndrome.*

- *Active shooter scenarios with law enforcement.*

- *High-rise standpipe operations (both physical and hose line use).*

- *High-angle rope rescue pickoff.*

- *Water rescues (swift and ice).*

- *Industrial Haz-mat spill (containment, mitigation, identification).*

Scenario-Based Training

> *"We don't rise to the level of our expectations;*
> *we fall to the level of our training."*
> *—Archilochus*

One of the best uses of scenario training occurred when I was in paramedic school. The instructor divided the class into working three-person ambulance crews. Each crew was responsible for checking off their assigned ambulance for the day. Our school had two older ambulances that were fully stocked, as a real one would be, for our advanced EMS care level. Each class day, the instructor would add or subtract items from the ambulance inventory and the medical bags. It was the crew's responsibility to find the error and remedy it, along with reporting it to the instructor. We needed to verify our equipment was ready to go. It was a great teaching moment. It instilled professional responsibility for our equipment, tools, and the resources we had.

You never want to find yourself looking and searching for something important when lives are on the line, only to find out you missed it in your morning check-off.

During paramedic school, our crews would be mock dispatched to various areas around campus, where the instructor and other teaching assistants would either role-play or leave a dummy or mannequin to practice on. Sometimes the calls were general and low-level; other times they were full cardiac arrests or strokes.

One great training scenario involved an elderly gentleman. The mock dispatch call was for a man that was confused in the lunchroom. We were given no other information.

Our crew arrived on the scene and found our assistant instructor sitting in the cafeteria of the college. He just sat at the table and stared off into the distance, as if looking for something. Every time we tried to connect with him, he ignored us and just moved his head to look behind us. We touched him on the shoulder, and he pulled away. We knelt in front of him, and he moved his body away. After about two minutes of the same routine, when we were at the end of our efforts, he started to talk, but he did not say anything that made sense. He would say things like: yellow, bird, oven, and storm. Then he got up and started to walk away. No one else was there to help, and we had to come up with a plan to decide what we were going to do. We had to act fast. He was difficult to deal with, and we learned a lot.

Dealing with difficult patients in EMS is a large part of our profession. Whether it is a geriatric (elderly patients), developmentally challenged, psychotic, or juvenile patients, we need to understand and acknowledge the differences and challenges that come with them. Our students need to know not all problems will have a solution. Sometimes there is no satisfactory answer. Sometimes we need to call for more assistance. We decided to call for security assistance (police), and then I also contacted the ER (our paramedic instructor) for possible psychiatric support. Depending on your area of instruction, you may have other resources, like a county mental support team for mental health or other geriatric assistance. In this case, my call for more help ended the scenario. The goals were achieved. We responded and evaluated the patient, tried to communicate and diagnose, and then came up with a plan of action.

In each class scenario, the assigned crew needed to accomplish the following:

1. *Crews had to check the ambulance and medical bags for errors and supplies as needed.*

2. *Crews responded to the ambulance and drove the vehicle around campus, having to navigate and find the patient.*

3. *They responded to the facility with needed EMS bags and stretcher.*

4. *Crews needed to locate the patient and perform a basic size-up and check for scene safety.*

5. *Figured a working diagnosis and established solutions.*

6. *Loaded and transported the patient.*

7. *Enabled IV access and medication use en route.*

8. *Used radios for communication to and from the scene.*

9. *Worked with the ER doctor and hand-off report of the patient.*

10. *Wrote a patient care report (PCR) of the incident.*

Once back in class, the paramedic instructor functioned as the ER doctor, and the crew would give a verbal hand-off report about the patient's condition and interventions used. All of this was performed in front of the entire class so everyone could watch and learn together. Afterward, the instructor debriefed the crew, and everyone talked about the positives and negatives of the scenario training.

This training was excellent. It gave a lot of life-like experiences to students who had limited to no experience. It used problem-solving skills and forced the students to work as a team. It hit all kinds of buttons for higher-level learning.

This type of training puts together many facets from didactic learning and marries them to hands-on skills. The repetition and the ability to slow down and ask questions allows for added adaptive knowledge and problem-solving.

Creating a scenario-based training program not only allows for varied situations but also gives you the ability to have the experienced members in your organization show the younger members how to perform on calls. Use all the tools and resources you have in your class. You will find many in your class who will have a great deal of experience or may come in with other diverse knowledge that you can use to your benefit. People with time on the job often are the ones I fall back on to help me in my courses. It also gives the veterans or experienced members the chance to demonstrate activities and how to accomplish tasks efficiently.

Scenario training is a great way to bring in those experienced students. This kind of teaching and mentoring helps veterans feel appreciated for their value and experience, and it enables the younger members to see the big picture as they imitate the veterans. For example, they may see how the operational placement of the fire engine drastically changes all the events at a house fire or some other high-risk event. They will learn the shortcuts to save time and energy. The secret is to work smarter and not harder. The mentored learning from this combined scenario training gives you more benefits than you might realize. It will allow you, as the instructor, to step back and watch the learning commence. I highly recommend making the effort to establish this type of training if possible.

Ultimately, where would you rather make mistakes? When would you like to see your veterans teach your younger members? As many generals say it is easier to sweat more in training and bleed less in battle. Make mistakes in practice and in training and learn from them. Be honest and open. Let the mistakes flow and let the learning and realization in.

As I've said before, we learn far more by making mistakes than we do by acting and performing just like we should. We remember the mistakes and we realize the importance of those mistakes. We grow and learn from those mistakes and failures.

Scenario-based training gives the teacher many elements to incorporate into one large-scale event. Everyone needs to understand how the cogs of the machine operate and how one wheel affects another. Students should understand what their roles and positions are in the scene and how important they are to one another. The instructor should relay the importance of staying in your lane and doing the job you have been assigned to the best of your ability. Freelancing, moving into another activity or following other shiny objects causes trouble. Your class and your team should realize how all the pieces of the puzzle come together and how everything is vitally important to the success of the entire operation.

Scenario-based training also gives you the time to work on low-frequency events and situations. Hopefully, by thorough and regular training and education of your class, team, and crew, you can take a high risk and turn it into a lower risk. This will enable everyone to go home safely.

Quality Versus Quantity

> *"Quality is more important than quantity.*
> *One home run is better than two doubles."*
> —*Steve Jobs*

Time is limited. We need to ensure that we are using it wisely, effectively, and efficiently. What is more important, doing something perfect for twenty minutes or spending over an hour doing half-effort incorrect repetitions? As educators, our goal is to encourage positive habit-forming. Spending twenty minutes doing it perfectly, or at the very least with maximum effort, is by far better. If all we do is practice the wrong way, what are we really learning? We are reinforcing bad habits and those are the hardest to break.

Working hard and working smart are two different things. We need to work smarter, not harder. Building muscle memory is important, especially when you are called upon to achieve at Two Dark Thirty. You want to have an adequate foundation to build more complex skills and knowledge upon. Being a hard worker is great. Having a strong work ethic is fantastic. However, we need to merge those concepts with doing it correctly and properly.

For example, when I was coaching football, we would often walk through a repetition or play a few times, stopping to discuss the issues or challenges. Then do it at half speed. Then increase to full speed perfectly a few more times. Finally, increase to game speed and try to be perfect all the time. Wouldn't it be a far better idea than asking the students to complete a task they have no idea how to do? Reading about doing an act and actually performing it are very different and challenging ideas.

Even worse would be watching them flounder for over an hour and get frustrated. The students might stumble upon the conclusion correctly. But did they learn anything? I know some would argue yes, the process of elimination gave them the answer—that they worked through the problem and found their solution. It might be true in some cases and in some activities. However, it is also true you could have spent the time effectively and efficiently by demonstrating, walking through the act, and then having them perform the act under your guidance. Wouldn't that be a more effective educational activity?

I'm not arguing we shouldn't challenge our students. We do sometimes need to make things tough and let the students get frustrated and stressed. Those stressful situations build character and memorable impressions of how to achieve the mission. This creates the needed situational awareness they will fall back on. As teachers, we need to realize when it is the most effective time to build these types of scenarios and training into the lesson plan. In my experience, your time as an instructor should focus on quality repetitions, not quantity.

Safety First, Please!

"The safety of the people shall be the highest law!"
—Marcus Tullius Cicero

When it comes to a scenario and live training with fire or other safety hazards, please use common sense and follow the legal rules. In the fire service in the US, we use the National Fire Protection Association (NFPA) 1403. This national standard covers all live-fire training. The established rules include all aspects a department or school must follow to run a live-fire scenario or training.

In my area of Wisconsin, we have several burn buildings and flash-over training containers. These units are specifically designed to recreate realistic fire conditions. They are heavy-duty and over-designed by very smart people. One might call them firefighter-proof. However, is not a challenge to see how hot you can get it! I've seen instructors burn materials that were illegal, like couches and plastics, just to see how hot they could get the room to make it more realistic. I've also had times when I've taken students inside fire rooms and let the fire burn for too long, creating the same problem. I didn't realize how hot it was until I came out and my helmet visor melted. Be smart. Be safe. Don't be macho.

When using acquired structures, there are different sets of rules. Here in Wisconsin, we need to pay for the testing of materials like asbestos and lead in the structures we'd like to burn. This is coordinated with our State Department of Natural Resources (DNR), and the city's insurance carries a policy for accidental damage to any surrounding buildings. It is also a nice gesture to go door to door and talk with any local neighbors about their concerns and the timing of the training. Remember, they will be involved, too, because smoke travels, and you will also have a large presence there in terms of vehicles, manpower, and noise for extended times. You might also have to shut down roads or street connections when laying hose from a hydrant.

Other times, we use structures that will be torn down for training. If we are not going to burn them, there still should be some basic safety requirements, such as verifying all the electricity, gas, and water have been shut off. Is there black mold or other hazardous materials that you do not want your students to be involved with? Take the time to walk through and do a very thorough check of all materials and issues that might arise. Do this with all the assistants and other aids that will be there on the day of the event. The more eyes you have on something the better chances you have of finding problems.

During one training burn, I was involved with, we had a very exciting time. After all of the evolutions had taken place and we did our final fire sets within the home, we allowed the entire house to catch on fire. All of a sudden we started to hear pops and bangs. Some live ammunition had not been found in the home and was now being set off by the heat of the fire. Needless to say, we found cover and waited anxiously until the shots stopped firing.

You never know what you will find in older homes that have been renovated numerous times. Whether you are using them for burns, ventilation, extrication, Rapid Intervention Teams (RIT), search and rescue, EMS, or any other training scenarios, please follow the rules when you offer these types of educational opportunities.

*"It's a very sobering feeling to be up in space and realize
that one's safety factor was determined by the lowest
bidder on a government contract."*
—Alan Shepard (Apollo Astronaut)

Part of doing any heavy work-intensive training should have a rehabilitation (rehab) portion. Rehab is important in the educational field because we get all kinds of students in many different physical states. Some students are young and in excellent shape. Others are older and looking to help their communities as volunteers. The shape and abilities of our students need to be considered when training. We can never assume a person who looks like a Greek god is able to handle high-heart rate activities.

Check students' vitals and ensure the area has a cool or shaded area where they can take off their heavy gear. Water is a must, and hydration will help the body cool down. Time is also a factor. Someone cannot be assumed to be in rehab for only two minutes. Your agency should have a rehab schedule established. If they do not, I highly recommend one. NFPA 1584 is the standard for firefighter rehabilitation. The Occupational Safety and Health Administration (OSHA) has similar rules and regulations. If a person has breathed down two consecutive self-contained breathing apparatus (SCBA) bottles, they should rest for a minimum of ten minutes, get in a cool shaded area, hydrate, and check their vitals.

Obviously, this will require the paperwork to track your students. On the book website, I have further materials you can print out for rehab.

Prevent accidental deaths, injuries, and training tragedies by following the rules and having a safety plan. Never assume. Always check on your students and see how things are going. Double-check the rope harnesses, and make sure everyone is paying attention to the little things. The details matter.

Your assistants should also take these items seriously. Ensure everyone is on the same page. Have communications set up and have a backup plan if the radio communications go out. Have a safety meeting with the instructors and assistants separately to go over the entire situation, and then have a safety meeting with the students to go over the expectations and the dangers. Appoint stand-by crews. Notify anyone else who should be or could be involved if something goes wrong.

Many terrible incidents can happen when performing these real-world educational opportunities. People die and get injured every year in training accidents. They are a fantastic way to learn, but they are very dangerous. Safety first, PLEASE!

Recerts Again!

Like it or not, this career is filled with certifications. They include certifications for firefighting, hazardous materials, confined space, rope rescue, water rescue, vehicle driving and operating, pumping, vehicle maintenance, trench rescue, and high-angle rope rescue. They also include vehicle extrication, life and fire safety, first aid, CPR, EMT, paramedic, critical care, advanced cardiac life support (ACLS), pediatric advanced life support (PALS), prehospital trauma life support (PHTLS), geriatric safety, and instructor certifications. Hundreds of hours of continuing education training are required every year.

These certification and recertification hours are part of the job. They are set and have parameters that require hours in specific fields. Being an instructor for these types of courses requires less planning because they already have set materials and curricula, such as American Heart Association (AHA) CPR renewals, and so on.

The biggest and most difficult challenge to overcome with these pieces of training as an instructor is to make them interesting and engaging. Sitting through the same ol' refresher course, year after year gets old. Instead of doing the same thing, spice it up. Make it interactive, interesting, fun, enjoyable, engaging, and memorable. Change the flow and make something new.

As I talked about in the prepping section, you can make it what you want, as long as you cover the required materials and the hours. The rest is up to you! Create games and competitions among groups of your students. Bring in speakers to offer reasons why things have changed from the previous edition and year. Have a tour of a new facility. Think outside the box. Ask the students what they would like to see and get their input on what they could do during the training. See what they liked and what they detested. Remember, you can make it as easy or as hard as you want. You are the teacher, so make it enjoyable.

Mr. Hill's Notes:

- Look for teachable moments.

- Train on high-risk low-frequency events.

- Scenario training is effective education.

- Talk about the event afterward.

- Keep communication lines open and honest.

- Engage your students in the learning.

- Safety First!

- Celebrate mistakes and failures.

- Sweat more to bleed less.

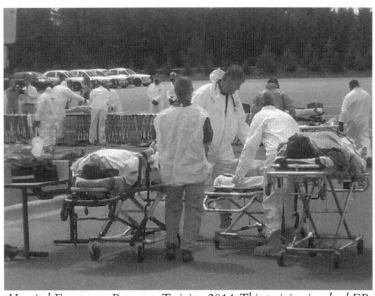

Hospital Emergency Response Training 2014. This training involved ER staff from two different hospitals and four other fire/EMS departments in coordination of a decontamination incident. Working together in a large event takes time, planning, and patience. (Photo courtesy of the author)

Chapter Six

WHY CREATING A TEAM IS IMPORTANT

"To ask someone to do something he is incapable of doing doesn't make him a better player: it makes you look like a bad coach."
—*Head Coach Lou Holtz*

In my fire department, the engineer (driver/operator of the fire engine) is responsible for planning and cooking the meal for the day. When it comes down to it, the engineer is the station chef. At least, that's how it's supposed to be. In my crew, we all have our strengths, and we all have our weaknesses. Some are just better at certain activities than others. Like cooking...

Early in my career, I was assigned downtown at our central station # 1 and had the wonderful opportunity to work on a crew with a fantastic engineer named Steve. He had terrific charm and personality. The room lit up when he entered it. Everyone wanted to hear his stories, and we couldn't wait to see what he was up to.

Steve is a great guy and a terrific person, but he was no cook. The man would burn water. Seriously, he ruined a pot one day by leaving it on to boil water. All the water evaporated and the pot warped and melted from the burner heat. So when it was Steve's turn to cook, we knew we were in for a special meal. He could only make a few items. Tacos, more tacos, or on rare occasions, spaghetti. The man of fifty years had learned to make two singular dishes in his entire life at the firehouse.

Don't get me wrong, everyone loves tacos, but it gets old after the tenth time. When Steve walked into the kitchen with his taco supplies in hand, we all looked at each other and rolled our eyes because we knew what was in store—but because he was such a nice guy, we didn't want to hurt his feelings. I even asked him once if he'd like me to show him how to make something else. He told me, "If it ain't broke, don't fix it!"

Because we all knew about his cooking skills we offered to help Steve with every facet of the meal preparation. It became a joint firehouse team activity. One person chopped lettuce, another cooked the meat, and someone else diced the onions and green peppers. Steve organized the cheeses and the sauce options. We all pitched in, and we all worked together to try to make taco day the best it could be. This also explains why he never learned to cook much in all his time in the fire department. Finding ways to create a team atmosphere can take shape at the strangest times and sometimes the most inconspicuous.

Being a part of a team has many benefits and many challenges. You need to step back and take yourself and your ego out of the equation. We depend on each other to accomplish tasks and to follow through on the mission. Teamwork is essential in emergency services, whether it is helping to make the meal for the day, working together on a house fire, auto extrication, or a pediatric seizure patient.

As a teacher, you cannot do it all by yourself. You need to rely on others to help you achieve the success you want to see in your students. Sometimes you need to ask for help, and other times help will be given. Either way, you must accept help humbly and use the resources available to you. It is never about you. It will always be about your students and their success first.

It is your responsibility to find out how to best give assistance to your students. In emergency services, we always work together in teams. The more you practice that with your students, the better off they will be.

Making It a Team Sport

Why did you become a first responder? What has led you to teach? What guided you to where you are today? The answers may vary from person to person. In my case, I've been asked, in different classes as a student or in job interviews, why I wanted to get involved with public service.

To be honest, we all have the same general response; we all want to make a difference and help people, or we wouldn't be doing this. As I was told when I went into teaching, you don't do it for the money. Do we want to make a positive impact and help the profession grow and continue? Part of being a servant is assisting the growth of the profession. Teamwork is vital. So how do we create the team mentality?

As a teacher, strive to come up with new ways to create a team among your students. Think outside the box!

We talked about scenario-based training opportunities before, which are great for involving different agencies or different classes together. These can aid you in creating team thinking. Ultimately, it is up to you as the instructor to create a team mentality. How you go about doing so will take time, effort, and planning. But the important part of a team is having people count on and work with each other.

There is an old acronym from my football days for TEAM: **Together Everyone Achieves More.** That is true no matter what you are doing. It takes a team to achieve anything successfully in this service. No one can carry the load by themselves.

Not one football player alone can achieve a Super Bowl victory. A football team has eleven players on offense, eleven players on defense, and eleven players on special teams. It takes all the players, working together with the help of their coaches and staff, to score those points, move the ball, create turnovers, and make a tackle. Whatever the situation is, everyone must do their job and perform as they have practiced and trained. "Do your job and stay in your lane," says Bill Belichick, head coach of the New England Patriots of the National Football League (NFL). Do your job, be professional, and understand your role; understand what you need to do for the team and accept responsibility for making it happen.

It works the same way in the emergency services world. As instructors, we need to impress upon our students the importance of working together. Tell stories about how you experienced success working as a team. Bring in speakers from other departments like the police, sheriffs, rescue services, air medical, water and sewer, gas and power, or street and highway. Watch videos of scenes and scenarios that involve the team and illustrate how important it is for everyone to do their job and work together. The best way to create team spirit is to involve the students. Put them in situations where they must work together and accomplish tasks together. Start with small steps and work your way to bigger and larger projects. The more you involve teamwork in class, the better off your students will be at achieving a higher level of skill and in creating positive social relationships.

TEAM Atmosphere

"Individual commitment to a group effort—that is what makes a team-
work, a company work, a society work, a civilization work."
—*Head Coach Vince Lombardi*

Creating a team atmosphere in your classroom can be a challenge. As a public school teacher, it was relatively easy because I had my own room to customize, where I could truly create the atmosphere I wanted. I tried to decorate my room like something out of a movie. I found ancient-looking sculptures and relics from various time periods; I even brought home a small two-foot sarcophagus replica from Vegas one year, much to my wife's horror. Historical flags from all over the world hung on the walls, along with topographical maps and geographic section maps of our home state. As it turned out, UV lights give me a bit of a headache, so I had icicle lights from Christmas time hung up across the room. (Ironically, I had to take them down later because they were a fire hazard.) Finally, I always played classical music subtly in the background. It was a calm environment and an inviting atmosphere, and it really brought my students into the learning environment I wanted them to be in. I set the atmosphere.

College and adult education are drastically different. You do not have the luxury of having your own room to create that unique atmosphere. As an emergency services instructor, you are normally going from department to department or from one room to another, teaching from a laptop or from your vehicle, using the equipment you have. It is totally different, and it makes creating that atmosphere a challenge.

To be successful, you will need to rely on your gut and your intuition. As I discussed earlier, you can start to create an atmosphere by talking and having the students share with each other in class. Setting the mood by communicating is the easiest way to begin.

Creating a team mentality among the group should be your priority after you have discussed your syllabus and expectations. When I am training and educating, I try to keep it social and fun. Truthfully, you really do not need all the fancy stuff I had when I taught in public schools. Having the right attitude is important and will take you very far.

As the teacher, it is up to you to set the tone. Start off by demonstrating how students can all work together by involving them in group dynamics and team-building events. Have them put a puzzle together with one partner blindfolded. Ask them to create a tower out of straws and marshmallows. Find an activity to get the group working and interacting together. This creates the small steps of the team atmosphere and group work that you will later depend on.

Sometimes you need to gently force the idea of teamwork. When I was teaching middle school, we had a spring trip to the State Lion's Camp for our 8th graders. Our school district had two middle schools and one high school, so before the 8th grade became freshmen, we brought the entire group together for some bonding and team-building. At the camp, they participated in all kinds of outdoor activities. Most of them were team-focused in nature. There were high and low ropes, scavenger hunts, kickball tournaments, orienteering, and water activities.

One of the most fun activities that students enjoyed was the low obstacle course. The course was simple. There were pieces of logs placed at different distances apart. The groups were given two boards of different lengths. The object was to work together to get everyone from one side of the area to the other. The rules were simple. If anyone stepped on the ground, everyone had to start over, and this included the boards. The challenge was that the log sections were farther apart and shorter at some distances, and you could not use the boards without using them together. This forced the students to problem-solve as a group. They had to talk, discuss, and plan. Natural leaders emerged, as they always do, and followers sat back and helped where they could. In the end, all the teams figured out the solution, and they learned a lot about themselves and each other in the process.

Think about what you can do to create a team mentality in your courses.

The team approach reminds everyone that no one stands alone. In emergency services, you are always working with a partner in an ambulance, or with crew members on a fire engine. You're always doing something with other people, and you never work by yourself. You must count on other people, trust them, and understand that everyone wants to win.

Team-building skills in class are great beginnings, but the culmination will be with those scenario-based training opportunities. The more complex the situations and incidents, the more they will reinforce the team mentality. Remember the old *Three Musketeers'* rule: 'All for one and one for all,' or the CRM (Crew Resource Management) pit crew teamwork organization we talked about earlier. Just don't forget that the teamwork mindset needs to be exemplified by the teacher and instructors first.

Cross-Curriculum Projects

Bring in your community partners. Think outside the box. Involve other disciplines in your scenarios and training opportunities. Create a team mentality by asking other departments and agencies to become part of your endeavors. When I was teaching in a public school, I thought a lot about how I, as a social studies teacher, could create better students.

Our school district challenged us to think about how we could get better at reading comprehension. How could we get better at writing? How could we get better at learning? These questions go beyond what a teacher can do in a classroom by themselves. It includes involving other teachers and other subjects. To reach these goals, we found a program for cross-curricular projects. We would pool our thoughts, actions, and lesson plans together as a group of instructors. I collaborated with the teachers in English, Art, Music, Science, and Math. We put together a team approach. We created class projects that involved all of us teaching parts of the shared view. The students were able to see how those different subjects related to each other and fit together like pieces of a puzzle.

We chose to start off with ancient Egyptians. Since I taught Social Studies, I spent my time talking about the history of ancient Egypt. In English, they talked about reading and creating mythological stories surrounding the ancient Egyptian gods and goddesses. They also studied hieroglyphic writing. In art class, they used the ancient Egyptian gods and goddesses for inspiration as they developed drawings and created sculptures. In Math class, they figured out pyramids in triangles and acute angles. Finally, in Science class, they made actual ancient Egyptian papyrus or paper. They even dissected a frog and looked at the mummification process.

Our students got a complete immersion in ancient Egypt across every school subject they had, and the students all benefited from this cross-curriculum and dynamic team-teaching approach.

The students learned more about ancient Egypt using this method. It was a very successful team approach. Just like in sporting teams, together we achieved more. As instructors, we developed and worked together as a group. We brainstormed ways to do things together and figured out ways to collaborate more.

This is something you can do too. Try it in your scenario-based training and education. Take the time to develop relationships with other services and subjects that can weave together.

For example, if you are doing vehicle extrication training you could involve these other disciplines:

1. *EMS with a dummy patient and longboard use.*

2. *Rescue company work around a patient with extrication tools or have them help with stabilizing or lifting and moving the vehicle.*

3. *Engine company to park at a protective angle and pull a protective hose line.*

4. *Law enforcement officers go through traffic control and lane closures.*

5. *Flight or helicopter medical air rescue to practice fly-ins, landings, and patient extractions.*

6. *Street or Highway Department with bringing in cones or automated signs.*

7. *Incident Commander working on coordination of all the groups.*

If you have a course specific to just one subject, use group projects and split the course into different phases so groups can work together. Find ways to involve as many other agencies and departments as possible.

A team mentality is not just for sports. It is something every organization can do, and it needs to be worked on because, in real life, it is what happens. We all must work together and depend on each other.

Making It Fun

If you are in a fire or EMS department, use your station house designs or catchphrases. Our Fire Station #2 is called the 'Vacation Station' because it historically has the lowest number of emergency calls and people chose to be out there to get away from the hustle and bustle of our inner city stations. I've seen some firehouses that call themselves the "Black Sheep". If you don't have these types of sayings and traditions, then make some. Have the class design a class slogan or a team logo. You can turn it into a team-building and bonding experience. Share what some other departments or agencies have for their station house designs or phrases. Having these tangible objects fosters a team mentality. The students become a part of something special, and they will take responsibility for their success as members of that team.

Empowering your students is an essential part of the team approach to education. Find creative ways to have your students contribute to the training and learning. For example, I used the participant approach by dividing the core refresher subjects into group projects. There were many topics I needed to cover according to the paramedic licensing requirements. Some required only an hour, and some required many more. To make things fun and exciting, I did as my past college professor did. I split the course into topic parts like cardiology, respiratory, toxins, trauma, and so on. I then let the students pick groups and then let each group pick a topic. To make this even more fun, I played a game of Jeopardy with them to earn points. Winners had the first pick of topics for the group.

However, splitting the class into groups does have its detractors. The last thing you want to create is animosity within your class. If one group dominates all the time, you will create an us-versus-them mentality and turn the entire class against each other. Make sure that the activity is fun and that everyone involved understands the end goal. Just be careful and make sure it is fun.

The groups worked out very well. The paramedic refresher teams took their topics and created a class lesson on that subject. They could do it however they wanted, it just needed to cover the required objectives for the topic. The groups came up with all kinds of presentations and activities that involved everyone in the class. Some groups chose to make PowerPoint presentations. Others used video segments, and others created fill-in-the-blank note sheets. One group made a skit. Their creativity led to positive outcomes, and the entire class had fun, learned, and participated. We learned more together and had fun in the process. It was far better than me trying to do it alone.

Think outside the box. You will be amazed at what your students can come up with if only given the opportunity to think up creative and fun ideas. The learning and refresher goals were achieved, and the course was one of the best I had a chance to be a part of. Making the learning fun and involving everyone in the process created the team mentality I hoped for. It also gave the students the chance to own their work more, which created a larger knowledge base for themselves.

Friendly Competition

"The way a team plays as a whole determines its success. You may have the greatest bunch of individual stars in the world, but if they don't play together, the club won't be worth a dime. "
—*Babe Ruth*

Admittedly, building a team was much easier when I was an athletics coach. In my time, I have been both a head coach and an assistant coach at multiple levels, from middle school to college. In those endeavors, creating team spirit and an atmosphere is easier, partly because you already have a team identity. Whether you are in college or in high school, there is a mascot. There are colors and usually a common song or rally. These items are easy to see and identify with. Identity is part of the sports mentality. How can we achieve the same results in our classroom?

In emergency services, putting your class into this frame of mind will take effort and planning. Friendly competition is a terrific motivator. In business settings, there are sales goals and targets. The first person to get to the goal usually wins a prize or a monetary bonus. As the teacher, you could do something similar with extra credit points, the ability to leave class early, or points toward getting donuts for the class.

Sports are straightforward. In education, you really need to put on your thinking cap and find new ways to accomplish the same team effect. Because we are teaching emergency services, it may be easier, because everyone knows they need to work as a crew on tasks. If you are teaching career firefighters, you can split them up by station or shift. If you volunteer, you can do it by region or age group, or you could let them pick their own groups.

Traveling trophies are an entertaining way to create a competitive spirit. You can organize the groups in the course to compete for who did the best job at a particular task or training day and earn the trophy. The trophy would be passed around the class by whichever system you create, but make sure as the instructor you create the competition for it to move around the room.

When I was coaching football, I would give out coupons to a local fast-food restaurant or an ice cream parlor. I would review the past game's film with my defensive squad. We would rate the performance together based on the calls that were made and whether the player was in the correct position and using the best technique. Points were awarded, and the best defensive lineman earned the food reward. At the end of the season, I tallied up who did the best job, and the best defensive player for the season got a steak dinner. As a teacher, you have a lot of pull and power to make it interesting and fun. Find a way to keep your students engaged and striving for their best together.

In education, the goal is always the process of learning and growing as a student. You want to create a team spirit within the class itself and not pit students against each other. Education is about learning the basics and advancing to apply, adapt, and use the information. Your lessons and the course should be set up for those types of higher-order thinking skills. Creating a team atmosphere will help you and your students succeed. Sports psychologists have often said in team bonding experiences, the team responds when they are found in a position of pain or near suffering. They must come together as a group and find a solution to overcome the crisis. In the military, they do this kind of training during boot camp. In special forces, some end their training with a 'hell week' involving long, grueling, sleep-deprived marches with heavy packs and obstacle courses. In emergency services, we share more emotional pain than physical pain, but the principles are the same. A hurtful experience is shared by all, and through that pain, we come together and finish strong.

A good team member will find ways to contribute. Sometimes, it will take the instructor to demonstrate this. Maybe students with more life experience can step up and show the less experienced members. It may be appropriate for a parent who delivered his own child to step in and explain more about childbirth, or a mechanic who to explain parts of a car, including where not to cut with the extrication tools. You never know where the help is coming from. Be open to it and relish it when it surfaces. Use it.

If a little competition starts to emerge amongst your groups or teams, know it is not dangerous. Competition breeds success. Take some time to fall back on those group discussions and interactions with your class from day one. Everyone should be on the same page. Competition can create an atmosphere of reaching for higher levels of standards and expectations.

Occasionally competition can get out of hand. As the teacher or head coach, it is up to you to watch and see how the activities progress. Friendly competition is great and builds team spirit. Quarterback Tom Brady and the NFL New England Patriots championship in the early 2000s always had levels of competition among their own team members. They were constantly trying to "one-up" each other. Who spent the most time reviewing the opponent's film, and who arrived early or stayed late after practice? Who was doing extra running workouts or spending more time in the weight room? The competition with their own team members forced a higher standard of expectation. The team did it themselves. The players pushed themselves and pressured each other.

Pressure creates diamonds out of coal. It forces you to adapt and overcome your circumstances. Creating this environment in your class and among your students creates an atmosphere that builds team bonding and a strong work ethic. Teach your students to rely on each other and push each other to get better.

Camaraderie

Working with individuals on shift for eight to forty-eight hours can be a colossal challenge. If you do it with a group of people you don't get along with, it can feel like an eternity. That is why a lot of the fire service deals with pranks and fooling around. Joking around is a way to relax in a high-stress environment. It creates bonds and friendships that are imperative in this service. You learn early on that you need to be able to take a joke or else you will become the butt of every joke and prank.

However, there are many states and regions that outright forbid any kind of horseplay or hijinks. They see this behavior as creating a hostile work environment or a harassment scenario.

I am by no means saying that to be a successful teacher, you NEED to have hijinks or pranks within your class—but I will say levity and humor do have a part. They can create a relaxing environment for the students. The pranks or the humor can be directed at yourself if you choose to take this sort of path. There's nothing wrong with a little self-deprecating humor to lighten the mood or to bring everyone back to the lesson.

The real challenge arises if you want to try to foster this type of activity and camaraderie. Television and movies show a glimpse into some of the hijinks that occur at the firehouse. I will be honest and say I have not personally started any of the activities, but I have played a part or two. It is an important part of the family and team atmosphere. The camaraderie and rapport you develop build trust and respect with your fellow crew members. If they know you have a sense of humor and can take a joke or give one, then you must be alright. That (plus being able to cook) is a major bonus.

"It is one of the blessings of old friends that you can afford to be stupid with them."
—*Ralph Waldo Emerson*

One of the best shenanigans I had the great joy of being involved in was when I was downtown at our central station. Central is the home to most probationary firefighters (probie) until they reach six months and get rotated out to outside firehouses. We had a new member who was a bit shy and was not the best at taking jokes well. So, obviously, the core mission was to get him to relax and become a part of the team. The entire downtown crew, including our battalion chief, was in on the planning and organization of the caper to get our probie. We knew we needed to come up with something unique and memorable—something we could tell tales about until we retired.

After dinner was our personal time. People usually start to go to bed at about nine o'clock in a large dorm room upstairs, where we all slept. We watched to make sure no one was still up and the probie was in bed after he did all his chores, and we waited about half an hour to make sure he was asleep. Slowly, one by one, we crawled out of our beds and went downstairs. We opened the station doors and took all the trucks out, leaving in their place our station boots. It looked as if we had left on a fire call; nothing but an empty garage with boots and shoes strewn all over the floor. We then hid in the station and used our radios to make it sound like we were already on a serious call. Someone yelled out hydrant locations and orders to pull a hose line. Our lieutenant did a quick first-in radio report of a building fire. We had the chief yell on the radio, "Where is the probie?" The radio traffic could be heard on the station radio overhead; there was no way he could miss it!

Our probie fell for it. He came running down the stairs, nearly falling, and ran out into the apparatus bay. He ran around in circles and saw all the trucks gone and our boots left behind. He ran back into the offices and then ran back into the bay, yelling assorted curse words. Then he saw the trucks were just on the outside platform in front of the doors. We all popped out of our hiding spots and laughed.

He did not take the joke well. He marched back upstairs, went to bed, and refused to talk to us. We all thought it was funny and one of the best pranks we had seen played out. He did eventually warm up the next morning, but it took him a while. We included him in other schemes, and he soon became part of the group. Even today, years later, we talk about it and laugh. He's become one of the biggest pranksters in the department. Doing these kinds of things helps to build team atmosphere and spirit.

Having the ability to laugh at yourself is huge. It plays a major role in emergency services and, as a teacher, it is one of the best ways to foster that type of teamwork environment. It also creates a family atmosphere.

Being in this profession, we always say our department family is our second family. We spend a lot of time with them and interact with them. A third of our lives are spent with these unique individuals. Some of us spend more time with our department family than with our own. We truly become brothers and sisters with those we work and live with. Having this family atmosphere is important to this job. We need to develop this type of trust, devotion, and faith in our coworkers. We need to know you are willing to give their lives for us, and we are willing to do the same. The camaraderie inspired by joking around and horseplay is part of building trust and faith. Encourage it in a respectful manner.

The team mentality is a large part of what makes this job unique and challenging. Those of us who have participated in group sports see how similar they are. Like a football team, we have roles and positions that help us do our own jobs. We depend on each other to put in the effort and have good attitudes. The ability to have fun and make the profession enjoyable pulls people into this career. We have a lot of stressful events to process from the scenes and incidents we work on. Creating a camaraderie spirit is a major part of the emergency profession, so make it a major part of your classroom.

Mentee and Mentor

> *"I'm a mentor to anybody who's interested."*
> *—Clint Eastwood*

When I was working toward my master's degree in education, I did my graduate thesis research on the role of new teacher mentees. During my examination, I found there were many differences in what people thought the roles of both the mentor and the mentee were. Some thought the mentor was a teacher, but just for the new employees. They thought mentors were to tell the mentee what to do or how to do it. Others thought of the role as more of a guide and a person to steer the new mentee on their way. Still, others had no idea, and they didn't care.

So, what is the right answer?

By definition, a mentor is a person who advises. Mentors are *a trusted counselor or guide,* according to Merriam-Webster Dictionary. The key word here is 'guide.' Mentors are not teachers. They are there to show the mentee the path and to knock them back onto it if they stray. Mentors are there to answer questions and share their experiences. They illustrate to the mentee through their work and offer suggestions for problems. They guide mentees, rather than lecture them.

The mentee, on the other hand, is a brand-new recruit who is looking to become a professional. They are the protege.

Many skilled tradespeople, such as electricians, ironworkers, plumbers, millwrights, and carpenters, have varying levels of experience and craftsmanship. These levels often correspond to the achievement and mastery of the student within the field. These students start as an apprentice and, through work experience and school, achieve the status of a journeyman. At that point, they have reached a level of professionalism that can be relied upon, and they have significant knowledge. A mentee is like an apprentice. Mentees may know what the job is, but they do not have the skills and knowledge to do it alone. They are a work in progress.

We must all start at the bottom, no matter how much we think we know or understand. Mentees are just starting the journey toward mastery. Their role is to make mistakes and to learn the best they can. The mentor offers help and guidance as the mentee gains knowledge and ability.

The relationship between the mentor and mentee is important. They need to trust each other and have an open and honest relationship. They are a team. The mentor needs to be able to say what needs to be said, and the mentee needs to accept this frank, honest communication with an open mind. This relationship is a team unit with the sole purpose of driving the mentee toward the finish line, to become a professional. Mentors also learn a lot during the process.

I took the opportunity when I was fire chief to organize a program to have our newest firefighters become apprentices to senior members. The concept was the same: mentor and mentee. The goal was to bring in new members and help them to become successful team players and contributing members of the unit. It helped foster a working relationship, and it also created many new avenues for the experienced members to impart their tricks of the trade. This type of program is a huge and important part of the educational experience for many students.

Mr. Hill's Notes:

- We all want to help, which is our common calling.

- Involve other subjects or fields where you can.

- Create the TEAM attitude: Together we achieve more.

- Competition can breed teamwork.

- Develop a mentor and mentee relationship when you can.

- Find other instructors to work with together as a team.

- Camaraderie will help cement the team bond.

Black-out Communication Training 2015. During probation school all recruits are taken through a black-out drill where they must find their way through a maze with the help of fellow recruits. They must also reassemble their airpack to put on and use to get out of a self extrication drill. Communication is key in emergent scenarios. (Photo courtesy of the author)

Chapter Seven

THE BEST WAY TO COMMUNICATE

"The single biggest problem in communication is
the illusion that it has taken place."
—*George Bernard Shaw*

The night I was introduced as the Fire Chief, and the first full-time chief was a difficult one. The prior chief was beloved and had been in the department for decades. He was from the village and was considered family by many of the members of the department. Unfortunately, he passed away unexpectedly after an EMS call. Sorrowful clouds still hung over the fire station. When I walked into the station during the tour, they still had black bunting from the funeral laying in the corner of the apparatus bay. The department was heartbroken and was still trying to recover. I was coming in from the outside with a mandate by the village hiring committee to change the department and make it more professional. They wanted me to raise the bar of expectation.

On my first night, I walked in, set up my laptop and projector, and began my introduction to the staff the same way I would as a teacher. I tried to talk about myself and my hobbies. I talked about mutual calls we had made together while I was in my previous department. I even discussed the history of the village and the fire department itself. It was all for nothing.

As you can expect, I got a lot of blank stares and hushed silence. Many people didn't even bother to look at me during the presentation. They stared at the floor. I completely failed at managing the first day and that first impression. A small vocal group of department veterans had decided they didn't want an outsider coming in and wanted to make sure I would leave as soon as possible. They disseminated that message to others, and before I even walked into the building, I had a near mutiny on my hands.

Looking back, I should have recognized the situation earlier. Politics plays a large part in most things in life, fortunate or not. My experience told me to investigate who the key power players were—to get lunch together and start to earn their trust. I needed to find out who could help me get the department back on track. You only get one shot at a first impression; there are no do-overs. I spent months trying to repair the damage I had done on the first night.

How you start your class is important. It sets the tone, and it is the first time your students meet you and you meet them. Make a good impression. Take the time to get to know your audience. Find out how many students you have, where they are coming from, how old they are, how experienced they are, and so on. That way, you can address some of their concerns in your first meeting. Calm their nerves and your own. It's all part of an effective communication plan.

Communicating and managing people takes a lot of skill and hard work. It is tough, and it is demanding. As we've seen people are all different and come with varied and diverse thoughts, feelings, and beliefs. There are many examples of what a good leader does, and many examples of what poor leadership looks like. I'm sure you have seen or worked for both types. It is a challenge to find ways to motivate and inspire. Sometimes it is mentally exhausting to try to come up with a way to reach your class members. I learned a lot from my failures. I often think back and still find it hard to believe what I have done or failed to do—especially when I know better. That is one of the reasons I decided to write this book. I would hate to see anyone make the mistakes I have. I learned from them, and hopefully, you can too. In order to tell those gripping stories in class and captivate your students, you need to be a great communicator.

Communication is Key

"All right everyone, line up alphabetically according to your height."
—Casey Stengel

You can never over-communicate. You can rarely give too much information. Disseminating information is key in any teaching position.

It is your job and your responsibility to make sure everyone is on the same page. Remember to engage your students by inviting questions. Work to ensure everyone knows and understands the expectations. This is an obvious rule, but we do not want to assume anything. The best teachers I've had and seen are those who effectively communicate course material and create a safe and friendly learning environment in the classroom. They have a calmness about them that invites questions and helps students relax so their minds absorb the information.

Communication takes many forms, from e-mail and direct communication to body language.

We all pick up on the little things. When sending emails or anything that is written, sometimes it helps to write them down and save them. Let messages stew a bit before you send them out, especially when they are to your supervisors or to a large group. Make sure your message says what you intend it to say with the right inflections. We write things in our own way, and it sometimes comes across differently than we think it will. It is always useful to have someone else look over items before you send them, or at the very least, give yourself a break and come back to them later. You can often pick up on your own mistakes if you give yourself the chance. Allow yourself time to circle back before sending those communications.

When you are speaking to a student face-to-face, listen more than you speak. As the old saying goes, "We have two ears and one mouth for a reason." Use them appropriately. You need to listen to the person and understand what they are saying before you develop your response and rebuttal.

I cannot tell you how many times I have had a conversation with someone who looks like they are listening, only to find out when they speak, they didn't hear what I was saying. Listening is the starting point, but really hearing what the person is trying to tell you is more important. Do not just wait for your chance to start talking.

The classic communication model is accurate. There is the sender—the person talking--and there is the receiver, or the person listening. Your message needs to be heard and processed by the receiver. This takes milliseconds for a receivers' brain to accomplish, assuming they heard and received your message correctly.

Think about all the environmental factors on an emergency scene. There may be people shouting, lights and sirens going off in the background, radio traffic, and family members talking and asking worried questions. There is usually a bustle of people talking over each other. The classic model does not take this into consideration.

In good communication, eye contact is key. Repeating or paraphrasing what you heard is also important. By doing this you are showing that you understand and were listening and hearing the appropriate message. Remember, in an educational course setting, your students will have varied life experiences and will have their own stories and histories their brains are working on. This impacts the filters they process your message through.

Your communication style can also have a direct impact on your message and on the receiver. The tone of your voice, volume, and sense of feeling you portray in your message matter. People can understand a lot from the tone of your voice. How do you convey your message through your voice?

Imagine being scolded by your parents. Remember the tone that they used, the intensity of it, and the disappointment that was projected through it. You can send feelings through your message and your communication. If you are speaking about something you find boring or have no interest in, you will project your lack of enthusiasm. Think about how you will relay the message. It is as important as the message itself.

A classic classroom experience happens when a student asks you the same question you have heard a million times. Take a moment and listen. The same question may have just been asked, but they did not hear the answer. Do not assume they were not listening to the other students. They may have been trying to understand a concept from the previous five minutes they only then understood. If they had heard the question, they most likely would not have asked the same question. Have patience and answer it the best you can, even if the answer is the same as the one you just gave. Be humble and professional. Remember why you are there. It takes patience, but that is what teachers get paid for—to answer questions to the best of our ability.

Attention Spans

Adults, like children, have a set attention span. In my experience it is closely related to roughly the age of the person. As a quick guideline, a 6-year-old can stand still and pay attention for six minutes, a 20-year-old for twenty minutes, and so on.

Attention is limited even more with warm or cold temperatures or if the instructor has a monotone voice that will put anyone to sleep. Coffee or drinks are also a major factor. How many times have you had to sit in a meeting or in a class after having drank a mega gulp morning coffee. You are antsy to go to the bathroom as soon as possible. Think about the last time you ate a big meal and got into a warm and cozy blanket on the couch to watch television. How long did you last before you wanted to close your eyes? These other environmental factors also will sap our attention spans.

As instructors we need to consider your student's attention spans. I try to regularly move around the room or keep myself moving on video. Shifting attention is the first step, but it is up to you, as the instructor, to make the class fun and interesting.

That is where your lesson plans and prep work come in. Be aware of the time you spend doing certain activities. Make sure you leave your students enough time to work on the assignments and be available to answer any questions that come up. Time management is imperative. I have found it useful to have a group interaction project or activities near the start of a break. Introduce an activity and give the students ten minutes to complete the task. At the end of that time, tell them they have the next ten minutes for a break to go to the bathroom or whatnot. That way, those students who are quicker will have time to get it done and start their break, and those students who may be slower won't feel rushed to get it done in just ten minutes. Everyone is a winner here, and you have successfully used your time wisely.

Also, be very careful with lunchtimes. It is far easier to assign projects or do evaluations before lunch than after. Afternoon naps and sleepiness are real issues. Have plenty of coffee or drinks on hand. Think about when you give breaks and how long they will be. Let the students know when to return! Keep a break short enough for students to recuperate but not so long their minds disappear. You can only have success in communication if the receiver is able to receive the message. They won't hear a thing if they are exhausted or in the afternoon doldrums.

Miscommunication and Assessments

"I love deadlines. I like the whooshing sound they make as they fly by."
—*Douglas Adams*

Late work is a great example of common miscommunication. Students should know and understand the timeline for the course. Discuss this in your syllabus on the first day. Your schedule for the course should have all the due dates for the assignments. There should be no miscommunication or misunderstanding if you go through all the course material together with your students.

Doing this in person is easy but doing this online can be a challenge. One good way to do this online is to have a syllabus quiz. The student must complete and pass the quiz before they can advance through the course topics. I highly recommend this. I cannot tell you how many times I have gone over the course information syllabus with my students, only to have a few try to jump into assignments without reading the material at all. It is easy to have a miscommunication when the student does not take the time to hear and listen to the message. It is our job as instructors to try our best to correct this behavior and ensure everyone is on the same page.

Besides assigning the work, you should also take care to communicate how each assignment will be graded. Every assignment should have a grading rubric. A rubric is a written outline of how you will grade the assignment. I have example rubrics on the book's website. It is hard, nearly impossible, to accomplish quality work if you do not know what the teacher is expecting you to do. That is what the rubric does. It provides directions on not only how to do the assignment but also how you will grade it and how many points the various parts of the assignment will be worth.

At the end of your course or class for the day, always sum up what you learned and what is expected for the next class. If there are questions, answer them then. You do not want any miscommunication about the expectations or the material. This is the time to double-check and make sure you uncover any issues.

Both instructors and students need an open ear to listen to what the message is. A great communicator is also the best listener. Repeat what you have heard and paraphrase to illustrate that you understand the message. In this way, there will be far less chance of miscommunication. These are usually assumptions and guesses. When I am having trouble with something or am in a hurry, I tend to only half-listen and guess or assume I know what the rest of the message will be. Stop, wait, and listen. Be professional and responsible for what you are doing. Never assume.

It's Okay to Say No

The hardest thing to do is to say no. In the 1999 Worcester Cold Storage fire in Massachusetts, where six firefighters died, the district chief, Mike McNamee, said the hardest thing he had to do was tell his crews to stand down and stop. Everyone was yelling and screaming at him to go in and try to rescue their friends and buddies, but he had to say no. He had to say enough was enough; they'd lost six firefighters, and he did not want to lose any more. Saying no was the hardest thing he had to do, but it was the right thing to do in the situation.

Sometimes we are put in challenging situations. As teachers, you will have students fail your course no matter how much effort and time you spend with them. It is disappointing and frustrating. It could make you angry, because usually those students just needed to devote more time and effort, and they didn't do it. We all fail at times, but we can learn from the mistakes we make. Life is about learning those hard lessons sometimes too.

My sophomore year in college, I met with my Electrical Engineering advisor. He had called me the day prior and told me to stop by after my Electrical Circuits class. I walked down the hall and into his office. He walked from behind his desk and closed the door. I remember thinking to myself, "this is almost never a good sign." He sat down and asked me frankly if I ever wanted to graduate. I was a little stunned and shocked. Obviously, the answer was yes. Of course, I wanted to graduate. He then said that electrical engineering was not for me. It was a slap in the face, but it was the hard truth. He went on to list all the failures and issues with my classes and my barely passing grade point average. I had been taking history and sociology courses to offset my failing grades in engineering.

He was right. Engineering was not for me. He then advised me to go to the education department and speak to them about becoming a teacher. I had taken so many non-engineering courses that I could earn a degree in Social Science. It was the best thing that could have happened to me and brought me to where I am today.

There will come a time when you need to let your students go. If you trust them and respect them, they will respond in kind. If you treat someone like a five-year-old child, they will tend to act like one. Trust the people you work with and give them the freedom to do the best they can. If you give students enough time to complete a project or task and they fail, it may be time to give some honest truth. It takes time and patience, but people do come around.

Take to heart the idea that you must sometimes say no to your students. There are limitations to this career, and it is not for everyone. Some people will take these emergency services courses and think it is just like what they see on TV or in the movies, only to realize it is far, far different. This is a cold, hard fact to some. As the instructor, you need to be real with these students. It is easier to do this at the beginning than to pass them through and let them become someone else's problem. Do not do that to another instructor or department, and do not do this to your students. Take ownership of your class and do what must be done.

We are all striving for our students to ultimately succeed but we need to be real as well. Those hard decisions may lead to the 'this isn't a career for you' discussion. Sometimes, this may involve a department's chief or training officer to let them know you have reservations, but you should always have a talk with the student first. Let them know your concerns and what you have seen. Be honest and open. Above all, listen to them. The lines of communication start with you. You can start by taking them aside and asking them how they think things are going. Ask leading questions such as:

1. *What are your goals for this class?*

2. *Why do you want to get into this field?*

3. *How have you changed your routine to make time to study?*

4. *What steps are you taking to plan for a successful outcome?*

These types of questions will not only help you assess their mindset but will also cause them to consider the answers and questions themselves. They might not have even thought about these questions before. If possible, initiate the hard talk in the beginning rather than let them coast by until the end of the course. Nip it in the bud!

Relationships

"You have to perform at a consistently higher level than others. That is the mark of a true professional."
—*Head Coach Joe Paterno*

Communication is also directly tied to your relationships with your students and fellow staff. It is important to start your course with the right attitude and persona. Your ability to develop professional and proper relationships with your students is directly tied to this. You need to be open and honest with them. Share your stories and be willing to reveal certain aspects of your life with your students. They need to see you as a real person and not a robot. This can be challenging in the online teaching world. It is easy to do in a face-to-face course, but extremely complicated in an online course.

For online classes, I filled the gap by posting a video introducing myself to the class. I try to be brief and have a set number of questions I answer as if we were together in the same room. This not only enables the students to put a name with your face, but also lets them hear and see you speak.

I assign all the students to create similar videos about themselves. They post them on the discussion board in response to my video. This technique link faces to names, and it gives the other students a chance to virtually meet each other. Video conferencing with Zoom or Skype or other online video formats helps as well, but also creates its own set of complications if the internet lags. Either way, the goal is the same. You are creating a clear communication environment conducive to learning and putting your students first.

Do Not Share Everything

"It is never too late to correct our mistakes.
And if we do not, we risk repeating them."
—*Lisa Madigan*

Always keep a professional manner. It would obviously not be a good idea to discuss with your students any personal and biased complaints. You should never ever minimize anything in front of your students. This not only makes you look less important, but it also makes people think less highly of you. Never put yourself in that situation. Never criticize students, other teachers, or other employees. It is best to try to stay out of politics or other public positions.

Avoid gossip and idle chatter. While it's important to foster friendships and professional connections, don't get too close to your students. Maintain your professional distance and take steps to protect yourself. Sharing stories from your family might help them see you are human. However, sharing too much can make people feel awkward. Just enough information to be relatable, then quit.

Keep it genuine and sincere while remaining professional. Some things are best left unsaid!

Body Language

They say nearly all communication is non-verbal, and this includes attitude. Your attitude and your persona will impact how your students interact with you.

Beyond attitude, dress appropriately and dress professionally. You should come to class wearing the attire that is expected of an instructor. Business casual would be the lowest level of acceptance. Jeans and basketball shoes with a ripped, stained sweatshirt would be inappropriate and would send the wrong message. Dress for the part. How would you honestly feel if you had an instructor come in dressed like a slob or like they just came in from a bender? I used to say in coaching, "If you look good, you'll feel good, and you'll play good."

> *"Language is a more recent technology. Your body language, your eyes, and your energy will come through to your audience before you even start speaking."*
> —*Peter Gruber*

The adage 'don't judge a book by its cover' is a nice thought, but let's be real. Our appearance is the first thing people notice, and we all make judgments based on that. Psychological studies have shown people will make a direct judgment of you within the first seconds of meeting you. Talk about a fast, quick first impression! If the book cover art looks interesting, I am far more apt to pick it up and look at it.

We all must be honest and real with ourselves, and acknowledge that we all make judgments, right or wrong. How we present ourselves is part of our communication. It is your body language.

The super-smart people who research these concepts claim body language accounts for over 70% of communication. It includes things like your eye contact or lack thereof, how distant you are from the person speaking, and whether your hands and arms are crossed or open. Are you sitting or standing, and are you leaning forward or sitting back in your chair? All these things provide non-verbal clues to others about your intentions. It is the subconscious sixth sense—it is something we do without thinking.

To further complicate this issue, cultural norms also play into body language. It is offensive in South American cultures to stand more than a few feet away while talking to a person. But in the USA, being closer than a few feet is seen as a close-talker and an invasion of personal space. In many Asian cultures, having direct eye contact for more than a second is seen as offensive and intimidating, especially for females. Waving your hand to say hello in one part of the world can also be a negative sign in another. If you have a multicultural class, come in with an open mind and do the needed preparation before class to see who your audience is.

How You Communicate

The process of communication is crucial. Beyond the message you send, the way you send it matters. As the instructor, you need to set a high standard for yourself. Create a welcome message and send it to all your students prior to class. The welcome message should be short, sweet, and to the point. It should convey the class title, the brief goals, and the intent of the course. You should also add a personal sentence about how you look forward to meeting them all on the first day and what they are expected to bring.

This will be your first impression for your students, and it will set the tone for the class. It needs to be short enough to be read and understood quickly. Do not make it more than a paragraph in total length.

Once the welcome is sent, make sure you also post the same message to the online discussion or welcome screen on the online version of the course, if you have one. If you don't, then just make sure all the students have the message sent to them via e-mail. If you do not have that ability, then you will have to modify it to welcome them on the first day you meet them.

How you communicate—and how frequently you communicate—matters. I have found success in the weekly reminders I send out an email and as message board posts. These refer to the course syllabus due dates and materials required for the course.

Yes, you need to remind your students of everything. It is easier to give reminders and communicate your expectations than to assume everyone will read and understand the syllabus or the course material. As the teacher, it is up to you to ensure your students are prepared and ready. Student responsibility is key and does play a major role in their success but sending out a friendly reminder will not hurt anyone.

The message you convey can be verbal, attitude-based, dress-related, or written, and it is entirely up to you. Make sure to communicate in the most positive and concise manner possible. Try your best to keep misunderstandings at a minimum. Your message should be concise, professional, and clear.

The Debrief

*"Everyone goes through adversity in life, but what mat-
ters is how you learn from it."*
—*Head Coach Lou Holtz*

A few members of my rural volunteer department and I attended
a flash-over and a positive pressure ventilation class. A flash-over is a
term related to fire behavior where everything in a room is heated to its
ignition temperature and on fire. The home this was to be demonstrat-
ed on was an old farmhouse with two stories. Other classes had come
through and had broken out windows and cut some ventilation holes
in the roof and sidewalls. The instructors of the class used plywood
to cover the new openings. Our class was to have multiple fire sets in
the home using traditional aggressive attack methods and then use the
fans to create positive pressure to attack the fire.

Once the class went through the usual safety message, our team was
lucky enough to be chosen first to participate. Our four-person crew
entered the house through a side porch with a 1 ½ inch diameter hose
line. The instructors had set a fire in the kitchen on the first floor. The
smoke and heat had already made their way toward the porch and the
open fresh air.

We crawled our way into the first-floor kitchen. As we made our
way to the seat of the fire (ignition point), heavy, dark smoke and heat
were moving closer to the floor. We knew we had a possible flashover

building. Just as we opened our water, the instructors turned on the positive pressure fan from the outside. Immediately, the rush of fresh air gave the fire what it needed, and we found ourselves surrounded by flames. There was no coordination between the outside ventilation and our crew on the inside. We sprayed water and protected ourselves as we tried to back out of the fire-engulfed room.

As we were crawling and backing our way out of the inferno, the hose line moved, and before we knew it, the hose was pulled out of our hands. People on the outside saw the flash and flames and blew the air horn to evacuate the building. We heard the horn, the signal to evacuate, but others took it upon themselves to pull our handline, our safety line, out of the house. With nothing to protect ourselves from the heat, we grabbed each other and stumbled out of the house.

I was furious and I was looking to hit someone. I wanted to know who the fool was who pulled out our hose line. No one fessed up, and everyone looked shocked at what had happened. I turned around and saw the entire first floor of the home was fully engulfed in flames. There would not be any more training today. The home was burning to the ground.

We were lucky. But when you use actual fire for training, there are rules to follow. The National Fire Protection Association (NFPA) 1403 standardizes live-fire expectations. We had no instructor with us at the time, and there was no radio communication between us on the inside and the instructors on the outside. There were safety flaws everywhere. I would hope the instructors evaluated what they did right and what went horribly wrong, took ownership of the problems, and learned from the experience. It was a communication nightmare.

This story illustrates the special place a debrief evaluation can have when communicating with your students.

As the lead instructor, you should sit down with any observers and assistants involved and discuss what went right and what went wrong with any training that is done. You should honestly communicate how the activity went and how it can be improved for the next time. Answer questions, such as whether the student's learning objectives were met or whether the scenario gave the right real-world experience you were looking for.

Once the entire scenario has been completed, you should do a debrief. Start discussing about what occurred and how people reacted is part of the learning process. Everyone involved in the training should be able to have some time to talk about their thoughts, actions, and beliefs. Record the conversation if possible or at the very least take notes. Some of the common topics could be:

1. *What are the immediate shortcomings that were noticed?*

2. *Were there any safety concerns?*

3. *Did any equipment or material break or not work correctly?*

4. *What further training or education do we need?*

5. *How can we improve this training?*

Once this is discussion is complete, the chief instructor should go back and change the scenario to improve it. Make it better for the next time. Usually, you can easily identify the changes that are required, what you liked, and what you would like to change. Write it down. Everything that comes up should be communicated in the debrief.

Training debriefs are also a great way to reevaluate how you have prepped and planned for the class. Reexamine your methods and use Gardner's multiple intelligences, Bloom's taxonomy, and Maslow's hierarchy to ensure you are educating your students at the highest level possible. Keep open the communication lines with your students. Engage your students in the learning process by asking them to reexamine your instruction.

Real learning happens when you can recall information, even the slightest vagueness about a larger topic, and apply that knowledge to an ability or skill. If you find you are training your students on something for the second or third time and it seems like the first time, then step back and reevaluate. They are not learning. Find the solution and fix the problem. It's most likely a communication issue.

After Action Report

The after-action report (AAR) is similar, and in many aspects, the same as the debrief. The difference is the AAR is done after an actual incident. Some organizations use the terms 'AAR' and 'debrief' interchangeably; however, the AAR is far more specific. It is a true report of an actual incident that lists the challenges and successes. The AAR can also be seen within the reporting software of any department. This can also be seen as the officer's report of an incident.

The communication involved in the AAR is also different in that the report is a factual and legal description. The debrief is a basic evaluation review of a training scenario. The communication styles are much different for legal documents like an AAR than a Debrief.

Hopefully, your organization has done an excellent job in preparing and training for the incidents you may encounter. As an instructor don't hesitate to pull scenario training from your AARs. These incidents would be well-suited for education and training development. Use other resources like the Fallen Firefighter Foundation and Line of Duty Death (LODD) Reports to find topics to cover in your training. Learn from other people's mistakes by looking at the failures of others. Incorporate those incidents as scenarios and as training opportunities. Some of the best learning is done from reflection and evaluation.

The written AAR has a few sections that need to be documented. There are many different ways to do this. I have seen many differences from military, to law enforcement, to Fire and EMS. Check with the departments and organizations in your area to find the best summary that your students may encounter. The four basic parts to an AAR:

1. *Review the incident. What was supposed to occur?*

2. *Discuss and note what did happen. Similar to creating a timeline of events.*

3. *Create a list of issues and challenges that were discovered.*

4. *Plan for improvement. How can we be better?*

A key point to either the debrief or the AAR is being open and honest with the evaluation. Communication failure is usually the number one problem cited in high-risk, low-frequency scenes, but we must acknowledge where the faults lie. This failure to communicate rests with training and rests with the incident commanders. We all need to realize that to grow, we should accept the life lesson, the learning lesson, and we all make mistakes. Students learn far more from a mistake than they do from barely trying, even if they are lucky enough to get out of a situation without failure.

Recall and Review

"It's not what is poured into a student, but what is planted."
—Linda Conway

Over time, everyone forgets things, and we forget things we don't do on a continual basis or have a reason to recall often.

We all get pigeonholed into a job function or a job mentality. Usually, we establish this for ourselves and create a situation where we live on cruise control.

In my current fire department, over 75% of our fire department calls are basic-level EMS. They don't require an advanced EMS paramedic level of care. The high-acuity paramedic calls account for only 25% of our run volume. So, even though I am a paramedic, most of my time is spent on basic EMS calls.

Use it or lose it, as they say. You forget what you don't do often. Spiderwebs hang in your brain, and it sometimes takes a minute to recall and remember what you need to do. Teach students to communicate that need with their partner. Talk with your students and let them know communication and remembering are part of the job. We cannot be 100% all the time. Be professional enough to keep learning, training, and staying up to date with current trends and best practices.

Communicate this concept to your students. Illustrate with them how you may spend time reviewing knowledge. Always be open and honest with your communication to get everyone on the same page. Communication is key.

Mr. Hill's Notes:

- You can't over-communicate.

- Make a great first impression.

- Talk about what is and is not acceptable to avoid misunderstanding.

- Think about your body language, look the part, and dress for success.

- Be professional in all communication.

- It's ok to say No!

- Remember to listen and hear!

Attempting rescue of a "cat up the tree" 2013. We tried but failed. The cat keep climbing up farther than we wanted to go. How you act in public and what you do is seen at all times whether you think so or not. (Photo courtesy of the author)

Chapter Eight

WHAT YOU DO MATTERS

"Check your ego at the door. The ego can be the great success inhibitor. It can kill opportunities, and it can kill success."
—*Dwayne "The Rock" Johnson*

My family and I were walking through a local store when, out of the corner of my eye, I saw one of the veteran members from my former Fire Chief experience. He saw me, too. At first, I wanted to pretend I didn't recognize him and just continue on my way, but I knew he saw me. I could tell by the look on his face he thought the same thing. I took a breath, and I walked toward him. I smiled as I approached, and I stuck out my hand to offer a friendly greeting. He had a bit of bewilderment on his face and looked at my opened hand and, after a moment, shook it. I said it was nice to see him and I just wanted to let him know I was sorry about how things had turned out.

The full story of my first year as Fire Chief would be a completely separate book. The quick version is that it was a difficult time for the department and came with a lot of challenges. In hindsight, I was too aggressive, and in retrospect, I should have been far more political and forward-thinking.

When I apologized to him, his eyebrows raised. He hadn't seen me since I left the department a little more than a year prior. The last thing he likely thought was probably, "Thank God he's gone." I knew he was one of the more vocal veteran members who spoke out against me and the transformation I was struggling to create. I also knew I was wrong about how I had done many things there, and I really wanted him to know I was sorry.

I was honest, and I think it took him by surprise. He didn't say anything at first but then said, "Well, you know how things go," and he told me he was a week from retiring from the department. I congratulated him and told him I'm sure the department would miss his fifty years of experience. Then he said, "You know, you weren't all that bad as chief."

That surprised me. I told him, "Well, I appreciated it, but I screwed a lot of things up." He told me they (the veterans) also didn't give me much of a chance and they were against me before I had even started. I told him the entire situation was difficult, but I was happy to have had the experience; I learned a lot. Then he said, "We know you were just trying to do the right thing, and what you did was push us to realize the changes we needed." We said our goodbyes and parted ways.

At the time, I didn't think too much of the dialogue and interaction, but now it is very important to me. I learned a lot just in the five minutes I spent with him. First, I realized I had to be true to my real self. I saw him and I knew he had seen me. I didn't walk away from him and ignore him. I could've easily chosen the non-confrontational path and slipped away, but would that have been the right thing to do? Does avoiding those types of uncomfortable conversations make anyone a better person or a better leader? I had to check my ego.

Second, I chose the more difficult thing to do, acknowledged him, and offered my hand. That was a risk. Given our past animosity, he could've easily ignored me and walked away. He could have snubbed me, and he could have chosen not to shake my hand. Thankfully, he did not. He accepted my presence and shook my hand. He had to check his ego as well.

Third, I needed to apologize to him. In hindsight, I did not start things off well and it continued to get worse. I didn't have to do it. I could've just started with some fluff conversation about the weather, but I chose to start off with an apology. I knew a couple of things at this point. He should be disarmed, and I wanted him to let down his walls. I wanted him to know I was not the person he thought I was. I also wanted to have an actual conversation with him. Apologizing first released the awkwardness, so we could get right into the conversation.

Showing my regard for him worked. He was surprised, but he was also accepting and calm in his immediate conversation with me. I disarmed the situation, and we could talk to each other without going to previous hateful corners. This experience really opened the conversation and allowed him to return the respect I gave him by saying some nice things about me and our mutual history. He didn't have to do any of it. But since I had already disarmed him, he chose to continue our path together. This conversation became a beneficial two-way street. Even though it only lasted for five minutes, it made a big difference to both of us I think.

Check your Ego

You never know when or how those types of situations will arise or occur, but when they do, you need to do the right thing and not take the easy way out. Confront the situation and do it in the most productive way possible.

Everyone has an ego. As the leader in your class, you are in charge, and you are the one whom the students look up to. Ego can ruin your teaching career just as it can ruin your life.

Has a student ever been disrespectful towards you, or directly challenged you about a topic or why you don't know something? In those moments, your ego may want to raise hell and come down hard on the person—but you can't. You need to be the professional in the room, the adult among other adults. As much as you would like to rip into the person, you must check your ego at the door.

Remember, you are there to help students learn. A belief that one must be right all the time does not have a place in the classroom.

Trust me, I know setting the ego aside is hard to do. It will be a trial, and it will take time to develop skills in your communication and in your behavior to deal with the ego. If I can do it, so can you!

Checking your ego is only the beginning. Along with ego, teachers need to be humble. Humility says a lot about you as a person and says a lot about your character. If you have the right stuff as a teacher, you will welcome the humility that comes along with it. Being humble and giving credit where credit is due is also part of the process. People serving in the field of emergency services are in it to help others. These feelings and attitudes are the core of humility. Others come first, then yourself.

Be humble about your 'great ideas' and 'perfect lesson plans'. Share them with other instructors and ask for their feedback about how to make them better. Yes, you are important and yes, you are the leader in the room, but you must also be humble and share the spotlight with those that deserve to be acknowledged.

Be modest in your view of your accomplishments. False modesty and fake humility can easily be seen. These are not things you want to be known for. Remember, teaching is a team sport, and it takes more than one person to be very successful. You can go far as a teacher if you show humility and give credit to those who assist you on the journey. Tell your ego to be quiet.

The Little Things Make the Difference.

"It's the little details that are vital.
Little things make big things happen."
—John Wooden

Two Dark Thirty happened again late one summer night. Our local police department was in a high-speed chase that ended abruptly when the driver of the car lost control, swerved off the road, missed a turn in the dark, and hit a large park sign. The vehicle's speed launched it into the air and threw it across the road, hitting a large tree on the opposite side before rolling down a hill, coming to rest on its roof, and catching fire. Police officers in pursuit were on the scene and were trying to put the car fire out with their fire extinguishers.

Our Fire Department responded with our usual contingent of an engine, a rescue truck, an ambulance, and our command car with our battalion chief. When we arrived on the scene, the police had successfully used their extinguishers and put the small fire out. The vehicle was upside down and had obviously rolled over a few times. Every door and side of the vehicle were smashed and dented in. There were broken tree branches, glass, and plastic pieces all over the roadway.

I was on the ambulance that night. As my partner and I walked up to the upside-down vehicle, I saw there was only one occupant, the male driver. He was awkwardly pinned under the car. He had his seat belt on, but the sunroof of the car had broken out, and the vehicle's roof collapsed during the rollover. His head was now half in the vehicle and half pinned outside of it through the sunroof. The car was basically resting on his head. I tried to communicate with the patient, but all I could get from him were short gurgling sounds. He did not respond to any questions, and he could not grasp my hand to show he could hear me. Given his condition, we had a limited amount of time to get him out of this vehicle and to the hospital.

Everyone on the scene had a role to play, and we all had to successfully accomplish our tasks as a team. We couldn't stray outside of our positions, roles, or functions. The rescue crew stabilized the vehicle and cut the battery lines. The engine company pulled a hose line. controlled the fluids and looked for more fire. We did our best to stabilize our patient. The police were on the scene to control what was now a criminal investigation and to control other traffic. We all had responsibilities, and we all needed to accomplish our roles and do the little things that gave us success.

We had a tough time with our patient. He was alive but upside down and, in his position, we needed to get him out of the car immediately. We discussed the best way to take the doors off to get the victim. The rescue company took the doors and used high-lift jacks to stabilize the car and lift the vehicle off the patient. We cut his seatbelt, and he was slowly lowered and positioned on a longboard. We carried him to the waiting stretcher and brought him up to the ambulance. The color in his face immediately improved. He needed some major emergency medical treatment, but we were able to stabilize him and get him to the ER quickly. All those little things, the procedures, tasks, and abilities felt like forever, but it took only minutes.

The crews worked together, coming from different stations and on different emergency apparatus. We all did our part, worked together as a team, and completed the jobs we had to do. In times of stress, you fall back on your training. The hands-on training and muscle memory, acquired by repetition, allowed us to be proficient. Our staff was able to accomplish all our little things successfully in a matter of minutes because we put in the time to train in these high-risk scenarios.

During the crisis, there were multiple little actions that needed to be accomplished simultaneously. The people and the time we spent training to understand how to utilize the tools and our knowledge made us professionals. Our education made a difference for our patient, and because of it, he lived and eventually returned home with his parents.

The little things we sometimes overlook can make all the difference. Never ignore them. Small things can turn into bigger problems later. Remember, what you do in the classroom makes all the difference to people like our patient that night.

People in the community have high standards for the local fire department or EMS service. They expect us to be professional, to know how to use the tools they paid for with their taxes, and to act in a professional manner to remedy the situation at hand.

As the leader in your classroom, you are the person to remind students how important those little things are. You can demonstrate how one misstep leads to another. Teach students both the good and the bad.

The 1986 NASA space shuttle Challenger disaster was traced back to 'O' rings on the two solid booster rockets. When they were developed in the heat of the desert, experts did not account for a possible warm, then freeze, then thaw of the material in the Florida weather. This little thing was overlooked because the thickness of the ring and the material 'should be able to withstand the temperatures.' Unfortunately, the seven members of the shuttle lost their lives. Do not overlook the little things, especially in high-risk careers like emergency services. Lives depend on split-second decisions and actions. Crewmates and coworkers depend on each other. As the instructor, keep that in mind as you go through the scenarios and the educational material. The little things add up and they do matter.

Realize Your Importance

"No one can be you-er than you!"
—Dr. Seuss

It is a great honor to be a teacher who builds the groundwork for the proper and professional response of emergency workers. Teachers create the educational environments that make learning a success or a failure. No one in the fire, EMS, or law enforcement could be where they are today if they did not have great teachers. Think about yourself and your stories in this industry. Consider how you want to make things better in this field. Read this book with the intention to become better at your craft. Teaching is more than lecturing, and I hope I have done an adequate job of relaying that.

There is a teaching shortage today. Not everyone wants to stand up in front of a room and try to educate students. People who want the challenge and pressure of coming up with new ways to teach important information are special people who care for the betterment of others. Teaching is hard, exhausting work. It makes you physically and mentally tired. Sometimes even your eyes will hurt. No matter what happens, you are contributing to the value of this service.

Teachers need to stick together. We need to help each other out. We need to step up and hold the hands of our fellow colleagues who might stumble on the journey.

I cannot overstate the impact you will have on your students and those you are training. Your stories and words will be remembered long after the class or course is over. Hopefully, you will be remembered positively. Either way, you will have had an impact on those you were educating.

Being involved in emergency services is a gift. This gift can be painful and difficult to accept and hold onto at times. Other times, it's easy and fun to be a part of. As with life, good and bad things happen. In this field, it is especially poignant. It is very real, and it can be a genuinely life-changing experience.

There are not many careers one can choose to pursue that can sway the balance of life. Emergency services like fire, rescue, and EMS or law enforcement are ones that can directly affect many lives. Though I have chosen not to share details, I have been a part of many rescues that did not end with our patients surviving. We tried our best, and sometimes our best was not enough, but there is always an opportunity to learn and evaluate.

I have also been a part of many success stories. People I have taken care of are walking and enjoying life, and being a part of a family because of the work I did. I helped give them a second chance. I was part of a team that relied on each other to enable successful outcomes. One aspect of teaching is sharing those immeasurable experiences, those powerfully positive stories, with your students. They should know the challenges that come with this career, but they must also understand the great pleasure that comes from saving a life.

You make a difference through what you do. You should never take your own importance lightly. At the same time, be humble and have the integrity to always do what is right and what is in the best interest of your students.

Our lives are journeys that include maintaining and expanding our knowledge through education. Use the professional development that is offered to you. If you want more, find new resources and attend other conferences or classes. The internet has given us a major resource for knowledge. You can search out many different opportunities for learning. Use the resources available to you to help you be a better person. Without you there can be no class. You are important and you need to be maintained as well, so you can continue making a positive difference.

Training to Keep Yourself Healthy

In the emergency services field, we all get injured physically, emotionally, and psychologically. It is important we also teach our students they need to take care of themselves in all areas. This includes the mind, spirit, and body.

I never had an instructor talk about this. Sure, we had a general patient lifting and moving section of the class. Mostly, that just meant you needed to get the big guys to do all the lifting. There was no mention of body mechanics or of proper lifting technique, and there definitely was no use of lifting tools like a gait belt or the Hoyer lifting machine. I hope as you read this, you also realize you should have those parts in your curriculum. If they are not in there, then add them! Slide boards, inflatable lifting mattresses, mega movers and other types of lifting and moving aids are available. It is always good to go over the different items the students may see in the field.

This is a wonderful time to employ those aids in a group dynamic scenario. Allow them to drag the 180-pound dummy out of the bathtub, down a short and twisted flight of stairs, or with the legs pinned between the toilet and a wall, because we all know people fall and land in the worst positions possible.

Bring in a physical therapist or athletic trainer to discuss how to properly move a person or lift heavy objects. Every trainer I know is more than happy to discuss and talk about proper lifting and moving. They can also talk about creating lifting and workout programs to keep ourselves in shape. Yes, round is a shape. You don't want to be the lone person sucking wind when you are in a structure fire, feeling faint and out of breath. Remember, you and your students are the most important pieces of equipment any department employs.

Stretching and yoga were overlooked and not thought of much when I started, but they have made a huge impact today. Even though I have a strong core, I've hurt my back when lifting both equipment and patients. This emphasizes the idea that knowing how to lift to save yourself from injury should be part of a whole program. I always want my students to leave my class feeling more informed. If that is the one thing they take away, I'm happy. Proper technique will lead your students to a lifetime of pain-free and injury-free work.

This job is hard on your emotional and psychological state. Do yourself and your students a favor. Take the time to get them the information that will keep them from injuring themselves. I'll talk more about your emotional and stress health in the next chapter—the other hidden aspect that should be part of the curriculum but never is.

Patience is a Virtue

"Genius is patience"
—Isaac Newton

Patience demonstrates character and ability. Having patience is moral and exemplifies your personal courage, strength, and virtues. It is difficult to master patience, but it is also imperative when you are a teacher. The time you take to slow down will enable you to see a clear picture. It will take the blinders off and expand the tunnel vision. Having patience will create the calmness your students will both emulate and admire in you. This calm serenity will enable you to portray and instill confidence, showing you are in control.

I remember seeing an interview with Mike Norell, who played Captain Hank Stanley on the greatest firefighting television show ever, *Emergency*. He said that when he was preparing for the part of being the Fire Captain, he talked to many officers who were on LA County Fire. They told him to act like he had done everything a million times. Portray calmness and patience. Calm, cool and collected they said. Mike did an excellent job of looking and acting the part. If you ever go back and watch the episodes, he is one cool cat.

When I worked at Station 3 as the junior firefighter paramedic, we got a dispatch for a fully involved structure fire in our downtown corridor. Our engine and ambulance responded with lights and sirens and found a large working fire with heavy smoke coming out of the rear of the two-story-old brick building.

Our lieutenant directed us to pull a line and attack the fire from the rear of the structure. The fire had been burning for a long time and was hot enough to spread to the interior of the structure. We continued our attack, and all was going well. Our battalion chief ordered our lieutenant to make entry into the rear of the structure with our line and continue to follow the fire to check for further spread inside the building.

We broke entry through the rear door and encountered heavy smoke and heat; we knew the fire was still burning well on the first floor of the structure. We couldn't see at all. There was no visibility, to the point where we couldn't see our hands in front of our faces. As we made our way into the structure, we encountered debris on the floor. We stumbled and crawled over metal shelving units that had fallen amongst other heavy-duty industrial kitchen items. As we tried to continue to push our way through to locate more fire, which had gotten into the walls of the structure, we heard a loud bang behind us. We tried to pull our hose line but were unable to go any further the line was stuck. We knew we couldn't achieve any more from our position. We needed to turn back and try something else. As we turned, we found a large air conditioner unit had fallen from the wall mount into the area where we had just come from. We were lucky. We just missed having the five-hundred-pound unit drop on our heads. It could have resulted in serious injury or worse.

Our department saved the historic building, and the owners were able to rebuild their business. We were proud of ourselves, but above all, we were lucky. Many horrible things could have happened if we had altered our path by just a few seconds. I credit patience and composure under the pressure and stress of the situation we were in. We did not panic. We took time to breathe, reevaluated our situation and overcame our challenge.

Patience has its place no matter what is going on. When you teach, it is important to relay that to your students. They need to work efficiently and with calmness. We do not run on emergency scenes, but we do move quickly, with purpose. Never walk around without a tool in your hand, and always check your surroundings. The little things can add up and they make all the difference for saving or ending lives in those emergency scenes. Be patient.

Students who are new to this career must understand their lives, as well as the lives of their crew, may depend on details like being patient. They need to realize the value of patience and calmness in the middle of a storm. Teachers can help instill patience and calmness by introducing them to life-like scenarios. In these life-like situations, they gain the classroom experience and training they will need to fall back on in the muck of a true emergency. Patience is a virtue that saves lives.

Patience is a core characteristic of a great teacher. Sometimes this means answering the same questions, over and over again, with a smile. It takes patience to think about new ways to relay the same information to the different learning types in your class. Taking the time to go one-on-one with a student who needs a little extra attention after class is time well spent. Watching your students attempt to solve a problem and fail also takes patience. The time and patience we invest in the class bring the most productive results.

Normalization of Deviance

"If you don't mind, it doesn't matter."
—*Jack Benny*

You should never be okay with subpar performance. Accepting poor performance and ignoring the consequences is called the normalization of deviance. This gray zone becomes acceptable in some circles because the supervisors don't want to have the hard conversations with underperforming individuals. They may not have the ability or skills to have these discussions, or they have not done an adequate job of explaining the rules or expectations. Either way, they are accepting deviant behavior, accepting poor behavior, and accepting below-par standards. Teachers should never do this. Don't look the other way. You must always set expectations high enough to achieve and communicate those intentions.

Motivate your students to reach for the stars but settle for the moon. Setting the bar high and expecting excellence will keep your student's mindset focused and allow you to demonstrate how to strive for perfection. Push them to be better than they are. Great teachers encourage students to realize their full potential. As the instructor, you need to model the attitude that poor performance is unacceptable. If you expect more out of yourself and have that belief and attitude, students will notice and follow suit. Remember, attitudes are contagious. Illustrate what you expect out of them.

High Standards Lead to High Performance

Successful coaches and business leaders often write memoirs that include how they strove for excellence and held themselves to a high standard. High standards tend to lead to high performance. The group rises to a higher level of achievement when subpar performance is challenged. If the group isn't held to a high standard, students will sink to the low level of what is accepted or tolerated.

Think about a job you had and think about what was expected of you. Did you drive yourself to do more and be more? Did you take the time to ask yourself how much you could learn from the position?

I didn't always think like this. When I was a teenager working in the kitchen washing dishes or as a stock boy at the grocery store, I never once thought about how this job was going to make me better in the future. I never once thought the work I was doing was important or meaningful. It wasn't until I got older that I realized those early jobs taught me how to work ethically, hard, and determined. They taught me to work with diverse people of varying ages, to talk to difficult customers, and to have patience. We often do not realize what we have until it is gone.

As a teacher, I try to impart this belief to my students. I'll give them the old man talk and tell them how these are the best days of their lives. Sometimes it hits home with the students. Other times, when I see them later, they tell me how they finally realized what I was talking about. Sometimes those discussions will fall on deaf ears, but sometimes the students will hear you.

I recall the story of the old man walking on the beach, picking up starfish, and throwing them back into the water. A little girl ran up to him and asked him why he is doing that because it didn't really matter. He looked at her and said, "It mattered to that one."

In this profession, you must have high standards for yourself. Take the time to prepare adequately for the class with personal integrity and pride in yourself. Have the attitude and belief you are going to do well. See yourself as a successful teacher, and the positive mental image will take root in your mind and in your spirit. If you believe it will happen, you can make it happen—but you need to set the bar high. Establish high expectations for yourself first, and then lift that bar for your students as well.

High expectations have limitations, though. We cannot be at 100% full-throttle all the time. You will burn out and crash if you try. Keep in mind, you are only human and cannot do everything. Ask for help from others. Let your students assist you in class. Take the time to organize yourself and the message you want to teach. Hit your own reset button and relax. Step back for a moment to listen and watch. If you did the front work, the preparation, and set yourself up for success, it will happen. Sometimes you just need to let it happen.

Some of the best advice I ever received was to do nothing. Relax and let the cement harden. Be realistic and understand all good things take time to blossom. If you try too hard and run yourself down, what good will you be to your students? Monitor yourself and keep yourself in mind. Keeping your edge and your mental attitude is important. Explain the need for this to your students and help them achieve it for themselves as well.

The education process is meant to help make your students become better than they were before. As the instructor, it is up to you to portray life skills, communication skills, and examples of how to achieve those characteristics. Students learn how to act from observing you. They will remember how you showed them to attack a fire or apply a tourniquet. The stories you told and the lessons that were learned. They will think about how you led in class and how you took control of situations, and they will model themselves after you if you do it with grace and professionalism.

But be warned! If you are a bad example, they will do everything in their power to NOT be like you. That is a serious thought. The lack of control or the lack of knowledge will be etched in stone. No matter their age or background, they will notice how you look at the class and how you show up. Just like my own children, they watch and emulate. They judge you. If they see respect and dignity in you, they will learn respect and dignity. To be successful, you must watch out for yourself and think about what you are doing. Keep your edge and keep your head up. Always strive for the best but be understanding along the way. Sometimes you need to stop and smell the roses. Setting high standards is the least we can do as teachers. I've often told my students to remember one thing: _**we didn't start the emergency, but when we respond, all we can do is do our best to fix it.**_ Raise the bar and show your students that lives are on the line in this profession. Educate them to act in a calm manner and be able to work in stressful environments. Create situations where the cream rises to the top. That only happens when we set a bar high. Then, remember—no matter how hard you try, and no matter how much effort you put in, it is up to the student to get there. Motivate and engage them to overcome the obstacles. What you do does matter but you need to take care of yourself too.

Mr. Hill's Notes:

- Check your ego.

- Sweat the little things, because they can make a difference.

- Realize your importance.

- Take care of yourself.

- Patience is a virtue that saves lives.

- Be humble and honest with your students.

- Never accept poor behavior.

- Raise the bar high and strive for perfection.

Traffic Death Accident 2018. The passenger of the vehicle was not wearing their seatbelt and was pined between the vehicles when we arrived on scene. Coincidentally all the parties involved knew each other which made the situation more intense and emotional. (Photo courtesy of the author)

Chapter Nine

The Toughest Conversations Can Be the Most Critical

"There is a sacredness in tears. They are not the mark of weakness,
but of power. They speak more eloquently than ten thousand tongues.
They are the messengers of overwhelming grief, of deep contrition, and
of unspeakable love."
—*Washington Irving*

Death is something everyone in this field must learn to deal with. My first brush with tragic death was when I was on my first volunteer fire department. It was not more than a month or two after I started.

We got a call late one night for a car accident, a semi versus a sedan. When we were pulling up on the accident, I saw a logging truck and what was left of the sedan. The vehicle had absolutely no chance against the semi in the near head-on collision. The sedan was a pile of twisted and broken metal with plastic pieces and glass shattered everywhere.

Unfortunately, the driver of the sedan had been coming home from working the night shift and had fallen asleep at the wheel, crossing the centerline of the highway as the logging truck was coming in the opposite direction. The semi-truck driver was fine and had no injuries. However, the driver of the sedan was killed instantly. The sheriff's department was on the scene doing their investigation of the accident, and the county coroner arrived and pulled up his van shortly after we did.

Our chief looked around and said, "Okay, who wants to help the coroner?" No one volunteered. Everyone scattered or looked busy doing something else. Being the new guy, he looked at me and said, "Marc, can you help him?"

"Absolutely, sir!" I said and walked over to the coroner being the eager new guy.

"Unfortunately, we need to get this body out of the car, so you have to figure it out," the coroner told me as he took a large black plastic body bag out of his van.

I said, "Okay," walked over to our rescue truck, got our jaws and spreader tools, and brought them to the car. The coroner came over with the bag and opened it up next to the car. He told me to get as much of him in the bag as possible and to let him know when I was done, and he walked away.

I was there alone, prying and cutting this poor man out of his car. He was minutes away from driving home to his family. I spent what seemed like hours trying to get every piece I could into the black plastic body bag. It was shocking, to say the least, and I had not been prepared for this in any of my training or schooling. No one ever directly told me this was a possibility. In class, no one mentioned the carnage I would witness and must deal with.

At this point, I realized the fire service was about more than just riding around in big red shiny trucks with lights and sirens on. It is about more than going to parades and showing people all our fancy equipment. It was more than just having fun putting out fires. The job is very difficult and deals with death and tragic incidents every day. We arrive to help on the worst days of some people's lives when tragedy truly has struck.

There was never any formal education about how to deal with a death of this magnitude. The images become entrenched in my memory. I can close my eyes and I can still see everything and remember the incident like it was yesterday in every detail. The memory is burned as a permanent record in my brain. Having been in the service now for quite some time, I, unfortunately, have a large memory bank of this sort of dreadful scene.

As a paramedic, I've been called to the homes of countless individuals found dead or unconscious and unresponsive and I have tried to resuscitate them, to no avail. I've been called to homes that were on fire, and after we put the fire out, we found people that did not survive. The worst call was to an unresponsive six-month-old baby who, despite our best efforts, did not make it. Sometimes it seems that death is a constant companion in this service. An ever-hanging presence just out of sight.

How a person deals with death is unique. Tragic death and dying should never be normal events for a person. What does become normal is the sight of death and dying. After years of service, it becomes normal to compartmentalize your thoughts to cope with the scenes in your mind. You almost put yourself in a different reality or frame of mind. It is hard, and unfortunately, it's something that happens in this career. It's our brain's way of protecting itself.

Unexpected Death

"The life of the dead is placed in the memory of the living."
—*Marcus Tullius Cicero*

As an educator, you may also run into scenes where the patient is a former student. This has happened to me on more than one occasion. I have seen too many of my former students buried long before they should have been.

One foggy night, our fire department was called to a vehicle rollover into a ditch. As we arrived one person, a young lady, stood outside the car, waving us down. She was yelling and screaming at the top of her lungs, "He's down there, help him, help him!"

We passed the young lady, went down the side of the ditch, and found the vehicle on its driver's side. The car had been mangled and crushed from rolling over at high speed. Glass and plastic parts were everywhere. One of my crew checked how stable the vehicle was and made sure it wouldn't roll over on us. The other firefighter made his way inside and turned off the car. He yelled out to us and said there was no saving him.

We positioned our equipment and carefully flipped the car onto its tires. The driver, a young man, was half in and half out of the car's driver window. As the vehicle rolled over, he was partially thrown out of the car. His seat belt kept him from being ejected. As the car rolled, it rolled on top of him many times. He was obviously dead.

However, as we rolled the car over, I was standing in a position to see his face first. To my shock and surprise, as he came into view, I recognized him immediately. He was a former student. I had been his history teacher years prior and coached him in football.

Dealing with dead patients and victims will happen often but dealing with those that you had as students is especially hard. Those are the ones that stick in your mind and linger. As an instructor in this field, you need to be aware that this may happen to you. They may be students, or classmates, or even coworkers. These deaths are hard to process. It will not be easy but it is important to understand and acknowledge that this may be a reality.

Stress and its Limits

Only recently has it been okay to talk about stress and how it makes you feel. But the overall common feeling is still to not talk about it. Many people avoid it like the plague, even on the job. A lot of it comes from the fact we all have our own buckets of pain or memories, and we hesitate to investigate them for fear of what they may contain. We don't want to be reminded of the death we have seen. We don't want to deal with it, so we put it away in a dark place, never to be seen again. We try to forget and ignore it.

But it doesn't stay hidden, does it? It comes back little by little, making its presence known by our lack of sleep or our chills when we hear a musical tone that reminds us of the alarm bells at the station. It is in our alcohol issues or emotional eating. Maybe it's displayed through our shortened tempers and our quick reactions to the smallest situations. No matter how it shows up, it needs to be dealt with. It is a lit fuse that is burning never knowing when it will cause an explosion.

I once heard my former battalion chief call it his 'bucket,' and I have adopted that term. He said every emergency call you go on is like a small drip into the bucket. Sometimes the incidents we are involved in are drips, and others are like someone pouring in a cup. Either way, over your career, you fill that bucket.

Eventually, your bucket fills to the top and it starts to overflow. That is when you have truly reached your limit, your breaking point. That is when it is time to retire. Today's incident call volumes are filling these buckets up at a faster rate, yet we still hesitate to talk about it. We should be asking how we can take some of that water out of the bucket.

Our minor daily stresses in this field also take a large toll. The little stresses, or micro-stresses, we face in this career add up. My record for EMS runs on an ambulance in our fire department's three-day swing, or our work cycle, is twenty-eight. My partner and I were averaging eight and a half calls a day. During that time period, not even one of the calls needed an emergency paramedic ambulance. None of them were life-threatening, and none of them really needed 911. However, people called for help, and we went.

We tried our best to solve the problems we faced. Whether it was a simple "Grandma, pick me up" call or a nosebleed, we were there.

Staying on your feet and keeping the smile on can be exhausting. Doing this day after day can take a toll on a person's ability to empathize. We only have a certain amount of emotion and empathy to give. Whether we like it or not, we give in all situations. All this giving is draining and saps the life energy out of a person.

Combining constant empathy-emotion with a lack of sleep and being on high-stress alert gets exhausting. Coming home to catch up on sleep becomes increasingly difficult. The lack of sleep only compounds the problems and issues we face. Having a vacation to get some needed rest is rarely enough time to make up for all the lost sleep.

I love food and go to it as a stress reliever, and I emotionally eat. In my first three years on the job, I gained 45 pounds. I will say half of it was stress weight. We keep the things we see and do inside ourselves. We store it up, and it is hard to let it go. It is hard to relax. Sometimes it is impossible to do so, but I learned to look for ways to compensate.

As mentioned, I try to compartmentalize these stressors. I shove it into a small part of my brain and do not think about it. I think we subconsciously try to defend ourselves by disengaging our psyche. We section those feelings and memories off from the others, hoping the bad feelings will go away, but they don't. They are there just waiting for a weak moment for them to erupt and come spilling out like a volcano. With time, I have become less social. I withdraw from many social interactions, keeping myself away from possible stress and similar situations. This is something I know I need to deal with and try to work through.

The culmination of these issues can lead to burnout, anger issues, and depression. Insomnia and sleep deprivation are key factors that start the process of the dangerous cycle of depression. Sometimes I would get physically sick thinking about having to get up the next morning and go to work. I dreaded having to go to the job. I lost my enthusiasm.

I was burned out, and I was looking for a change, any change. I tried all kinds of hobbies, but nothing worked. Finally, I found writing.

Writing this book helped me a lot. I regained my perspective about why I chose public service in the first place. Writing brought back good memories and bad ones, but it helped me to come full circle and find the gift in giving.

"It is during our darkest moments that we must focus to see the light."
—*Aristotle Onassis*

Post-Traumatic Stress Disorder (PTSD), micro-stress, and mental issues are also rarely talked about. It is becoming more acceptable to speak of it, but it is still a faux pas.

The day I had an infant death call, our battalion chief organized our responding crew (Engine company and ambulance) to have a Post Incident Stress (PIS) debrief, or in some areas, it is called a Critical Incident Stress Management (CISM) meeting. The intention was to talk about the scene and to share our thoughts, feelings, and concerns with a trained counselor.

Do you know what happened? All four of us sat in the room with the counselor for about five minutes looking at each other, just waiting for someone to say something. No one did. So, after minutes of awkward silence, the counselor got up and said if anyone would like to speak to her individually, we could, and she gave us all her business cards and left.

To my knowledge, no one called, not even myself. I regret that. I wish I had the courage to say seeing that little baby in the condition it was in and trying to bring it back to life was the absolute worst day of my life. I would have liked to have told everyone that I replayed that event in my head many times. I have trouble even now during our Pediatric Advanced Life Support (PALS) class. I can't see or touch the infant practice dummies without getting shivers and without having thoughts of the death scene, but I don't say anything, and I push myself forward.

I wish I had had a teacher or mentor that talked about this when I was going to school. I hope you are that teacher. Have the courage to address this issue with your students. Bring in the specialists. Have the resources for your students available for them to take home and keep when they get a job in this field. Give them the tools to deal with these issues in a constructive and positive way. Remember, you are not expected to have all the answers, but we can try to help our students find the answers or what they are looking for.

I never thought about the mental imagery I would see. I never thought about how much a person could interact with trauma during their time in this career. As you are filling the bucket, it is hard to not bring home pain and stress. No one ever taught me how to deal with the images and memories we can never forget. When we bring home our anger, exhaustion, short temper, mood, and attitude, we affect those we love. It is hard on them. Attitudes are contagious.

Why we do not talk about this in class is a mystery. This goes directly with our lack of education and knowledge of the ways to cope with these types of challenges and is the reason for the higher levels of divorce in our profession.

Students need to be educated about these types of problems and issues. More firefighters and police are killed by suicide than in the line of duty. Firefighters die of heart disease more than anything else. As we now know, scientifically, stress is directly linked to heart problems.

As teachers, I hope you choose to bring this forward and start honest conversations with our students. We need to talk to them more about our own health and bring it out into the light.

Recently, there have been many advances in this thinking. Many professional union groups, like the International Association of Firefighters (IAFF), have formed stress management groups and therapy recovery housing options. But problems remain because of the shadow of masculinity and the type-A "I can do it all and handle anything" macho attitudes that run rampant in emergency services. Many are too proud to accept help or look for it. As with my experience during the stress debrief, most of us just look at each other and say nothing.

Take the time in your classes to talk about this. Ask questions and try to answer them. The first step in any journey is the hardest.

Ways to Cope

Disclaimer: I am in no way a licensed therapist, psychologist, counselor, or mental health professional. What I've done is deep-dive research into this subject. I have found several interesting studies. I have also tried many of these coping techniques myself. Some have worked and some of them are a work in progress. It is up to you and they are all options. Either way, I implore you to try them and to discuss them with your students.

The main topic—how to deal with stress in emergency services—has been a tough one to tackle. There are many studies that have focused solely on grief, depression, and stress, but they rely on information gathered from everyday people and not emergency responders.

This is not to say those in emergency services are not normal, but you must admit not everyone is willing to run into a burning building to save people rather than run out. Emergency services are a different breed and we come with different coping mechanisms, management, attitudes, and grief skills that the average person might not possess nor would ever need to. Psychological studies of actual firefighters or EMTs have been rare, and the ones that have been done are not a statistical number you could truly say is a normal average. The studies generally only have a hundred or fewer participants. Given that in the United States alone, we have more than 5 million firefighters, a study of a hundred is not a very large statistical number.

"You do learn how to cope from those who are coping."
—Matthew Desmond

In my opinion, I think this goes back to our tough, strong, 'type-A' personalities. We don't want to admit to having a problem we can't solve ourselves. Therefore, why would we participate in a study admitting we have a problem? The way we cope with the continued stress we face is paramount to the longevity of our careers. How you deal with it does matter. What follows is a compilation, as coping will be different for every person individually. Perhaps one or more of these strategies will be something new to try for you or your students.

Weighted Blankets

One study I found dealt with having a weighted blanket. The weight is supposed to give you the feeling of being hugged and embraced. This, in turn, releases certain endorphins and allows you to process stress and stressful emotions better. The weights can differ, and the type of weight used in the blanket can also be different from beads to thicker material. I have seen some firehouses that have a bunch of them with their recliners. My wife bought me one for Christmas and I have to say I enjoy it. Plus, it keeps me warm!

Playing Games

A British study (10) found playing games like Tetris, which involve puzzles, help your brain digest and process stress and painful memories. This processing allows you to handle the same types of events without having flashbacks or having PTSD issues in the future. The catch to this was that to have success, you needed to play the games within a few hours of the event to have the maximum effect.

I don't need any more reasons to play games at work. If it works, it works, and at least you've become a little smarter in the process. Other computer or video games have helped, too. The important factor is that the games are simple and coordinate with eye movement and trying to figure out patterns. Games such as Candy Crush, Tetris, Angry Birds, Fruit Ninja, Flow Free, and the like.

How many times have you just wanted to sit down and turn on the TV? It is a bit mind-numbing. I have found that when I find it hard to sleep, I turn on the television and watch something. Within minutes, I am tired, and I have a hard time keeping my eyes open. These types of multimedia can have a numbing effect on your brain that allows us to step back and process them. Much like the Tetris study, these types of activities help the brain use other centers to process the stressors and memories that cause PTSD-type issues. Playing video games has also been successful at giving high levels of enjoyment. I have a sense of accomplishment when I play games and achieve levels and rewards.

Weightlifting and Working Out

One technique I'm sure you have heard of is physical activity or weightlifting. This is supposed to help your body process the feelings by working them out, literally. As humans, we store our stress and carry it with us both mentally and physically. Like neck pain and knots, we feel it in our muscles. To work the stress out, we need to do just that. We must force ourselves to operate our muscles and get stress out of the body. Lifting weights or running or any kind of physical activity releases hormones, endorphins, and good stress chemicals that help our body process those bad feelings. I personally feel better after lifting heavy weights or going for a longer jog.

Saunas and hot tubs are also beneficial for destressing your body. The warm temperatures help to relax the muscles and tendons after working out or after coming home from a shift. Finding ways to help your body physically de-stress is also important and not to be overlooked. It's not just your mind. Your body counts, too, and is often the first indicator of needed change.

Getting Out in Nature

Being outdoors also helps. Whether you enjoy hunting, fishing, hiking, photography, or camping, get into the woods or the outdoors near you and become one with nature. My fishing friends always tell me it isn't about catching fish, it's about fishing.

I thought this was weird at first, but they are right. It is about enjoying the moment, and there really is something special and tranquil about sitting in a boat with a fishing line out, just calming your mind. I enjoy hiking in the woods, too. I'm lucky enough to live right next to a state park where there are multiple trails that go on for miles. I often go on these hikes and take the time to stop and listen to the birds and feel the breezes. This may sound a bit New Age, but it helps, and it helps me relax. Enjoy the outdoors.

Animals have been known to have a therapeutic effect on people. Many stations have dogs or even cats in the firehouse to help with their calming manner. I have even seen some departments allow their workers to bring in their own pets. Therapy animals, and specially trained anxiety service animals, all have a special place in coping strategies. I was on a recent trip to the Grand Canyon and my daughters wanted to ride horses. I found a great ranch nearby. The owner of the ranch was a military veteran. He told me all about the uniqueness of how horses can sense pain and stress in humans. He was born in Northern California and grew up with horses and understood the power and special ability that they have. He bought all of his horses as rescues and uses them to help others, especially emergency service, and military veterans with their PTSD. I have to admit standing and brushing them did make me feel better.

Traveling and Family

Get out of your city and travel someplace you have always wanted to see. Take a cruise. Take a road trip. There are many places and sites right next to us we often overlook. Become a tourist in your own town. Visit a new restaurant. See the sights and go to a museum. People were not meant to be cooped up in buildings under UV lights all day. Enjoy the world we have. Go on an adventure.

Spend quality time with your family and friends. While you are traveling and looking to take a vacation include your loved ones in your plans. They are your first family and the ones that truly care about you. Include them and spend time with them. Sometimes it can be as simple as a phone call or having lunch.

Journaling or Writing

Other studies show some people find solace in journaling. Write down your thoughts and feelings associated with the stressful events and the bad feelings they cause. The act of writing can be therapeutic by helping you release ideas and images and get them out of your head. The writing you do helps to process what you are thinking and feeling.

I personally found this to be true while I was writing this book. When I was writing the stories, I recalled the events. Taking it from my mind and putting them on paper has helped me process the events and the memories.

This type of therapy is also directly related to talking therapy and verbal discussions. These coping strategies involve a psychiatrist or therapist. The sessions have the same outcome as journaling in that they are meant to get the thoughts, ideas, and stressors out of your mind. They are intended to start treating the cause of the pain and anguish. Speaking to someone can help you find resolutions and positive ways to understand why you feel the way you do. These sessions can help you associate your feelings and thoughts with productive patterns. Sometimes we just literally need to get these things off our chest and have someone listen.

Art and Music

Art and music therapy have also been shown to be positive. Find something artistic you enjoy. Whether it is sculpting with clay, watercolors, enamel paints, woodworking, sewing or crafting, drawing, metalwork, welding, singing, guitar, or other musical instruments, finding something that uses the creative side of your brain to help cope with stress is the answer. Find a quiet place to relax and listen to music. The sounds of waves at the beach, or the rain in a forest. It can be one thing, or it can be multiple activities. Being involved in art or music will help you process those feelings and stressors.

Consider whether finding comfort in doing a hobby leads you to better and more positive coping strategies. Set time for yourself to do what you love. If you have had a hard day and need to decompress, take the time to communicate with your loved ones about what you need.

Your loved ones will benefit. Support is a major factor in the successful outcomes of all these coping strategies.

Religion and Worship

Many find comfort and escape in religion and worship services. There are several members of my department that are extremely religious and hold their own Bible studies and workshops. Faith is something that can motivate us to seek meaning and to steer ourselves in a positive direction. The act of prayer also has had beneficial effects on a person's mood and attitude.

A lot of departments have chaplains that are there to work through these types of stress issues and are specially trained to handle stress crises. If you do not have someone in that capacity, then any religious organization has time for you. Stop in, call, or ask around. I know this type of prayerful searching can lead many to hope and accomplishment.

Negative Routes and Turning to the 'Easy Fix'

Unfortunately, many turn to negative coping strategies. An obvious one is alcohol and drugs. They are not the painkillers we may think they are and are never the answer to any question. People sometimes rely on quick fixes and what they see to escape from what is hurting and ailing them. This is understandable. However, using illegal or legal medications and drugs to escape leads to disaster, and it hurts more people than just yourself. Others rely on you and care about you, whether you think so or not. The quick high you may get from using drugs only lasts for a short time, and your problems and stress will be there to greet you when you come back down.

Alcoholism runs in my family. I personally never got into drinking and didn't like the taste of beer or wine, but what I will tell you is I love candy! Give me a bag of gummy bears and I'm a happy camper.

If you think about it scientifically, what am I predisposed to loving? SUGAR! Alcohol has a ton of sugar in it. Instead of drinking, I've become addicted to candy. I admit I have times when I crave certain candies. But as the saying goes, a little goes a long way. If you think you are replacing one thing with another, think twice. Stress eating or drinking is not filling that hole in your heart, soul, or head. It is just making things worse. Find more productive ways to process and deal with stress.

Remember, anything in excess is bad. Even the more positive coping strategies I mentioned can be bad if you do them too much. If you are spending all your free time driven and obsessed with a single activity, forgetting your friends and family, this is a sign of a real issue. Seclusion and hiding are key signs you may have a problem. This path leads down a dark rabbit hole.

"Nothing is impossible,
the word itself says I'm possible!"
—Audrey Hepburn

Although this is personal for all of us, this is about helping students understand that when the going gets tough, the weight of the world isn't all on their shoulders. They are not alone. There are many people there to support them through tough times. Help students avoid becoming a statistic. Teach them to ask for help and reach out.

Finding a balance between work and home is the key. Knowing there are ways to cope and deal with work stress is very important. We need to educate our students that death and dealing with stressful situations and memories will be a large part of their careers. One of the most important things you can do as a first responder and emergency services educator is to provide tools for them to navigate these stressors in a healthy and safe manner.

Guilt, Shame, and Disgrace

When it comes to dealing with death and its major stressors, I think a lot of the problems occur when we have guilt and shame. We are doers, we are fighters, and we win. We abhor losing. We push ourselves and sacrifice to achieve victory. The Spartan phrase, "*With your shield or upon it,*" duly reflects our thinking. Either you come back victorious, or you die trying.

We are prepared to put our own lives on the line to save the lives of our community members and teammates. Not many professions have this mentality. Not many people have the will or the ability to make that choice. I think because of this attitude and the environment we work in it is especially difficult for us to lose. There are times when a cardiac arrest or pulseless non-breather (PNB) patient is not resuscitated, or we may try our best to stop the bleeding from a trauma incident, only to find out they died later in the ER. It is tough to take, to put all your energy and spirit into accomplishing a task, only to fail.

It was a warm summer day, and I was taking my lunch break on the roof of our Central Fire Station, sitting in the sun, and imagining myself on a Florida beach when the alarm bell went off. I ran downstairs and put my gear on. We were being dispatched to a vehicle fire and a multiple-car accident. While en route to the call, our 911 dispatch center advised the vehicle fire had been put out by the police, but the driver was still inside the car. When we arrived, we found a vehicle smashed up against a parked car in a parking lot. The vehicle was still smoking from where the fire had burned underneath it. There was an obvious trail of black, charred marks that led from the roadway, across the street, up over the curb, and into the parking lot where the vehicle had smashed by six other vehicles. It was lunch hour, and there were many bystanders trying to help the driver and others just trying to see what the commotion was about.

I was on the ambulance that day so our concern was the driver's condition. My partner and I ran up to the vehicle and found an elderly gentleman. His clothes and face were soot-stained from the fire. I couldn't tell if he was still breathing. My partner opened the driver's door, and we grabbed him and got him out of the car quickly. We didn't know if the car would start on fire again, so we carried our patient a few feet away and laid him on the cement of the parking lot. We began our treatment. He was not breathing and had no pulse. We started CPR right away and cut his shirt off.

As my partner and I were focused on our patient, we did not notice or think about all the bystanders or other people walking around. Before I knew it, there was a large group of people who had formed a near circle around us, some with their phones out, recording us. Our battalion chief sprang to action and grabbed a few police officers who took the sheets from the stretcher and made a privacy wall around us and told everyone to please leave. While we were hard at work, we got the patient back! He had a pulse and was breathing. He even started to resist the endotracheal (breathing) tube which we placed in for fear of his airway closing, as we didn't know if he had burn injuries from the fire in his trachea or what issues he may have had from the fire burning. We decided to sedate him and put him to sleep.

We loaded him up and drove with lights and sirens to the ER. While we went, he coded on us (his heart stopped) once, but we got him back again. We arrived at the ER and got him into the trauma bay. Within a minute or two of being in the ER, his heart stopped again. The ER staff looked at the doctor who was checking the patient. There was no effort made to bring him back. The time of death was called and the doctor looked at me as if to say, "Why did you try so hard?" and left the room.

To say I was disappointed was an understatement. I was devastated. All the skill and effort we used to get him to the ER to save him was for nothing. In the eyes of the ER doctor, I wasted time and effort. He was an 85-year-old man who had a chronic cardiac issue while he was driving home for lunch. During the initial heart attack, he lost control of his vehicle, swerved out of his lane, struck another car, and ran over the curb and street sign. The street sign sliced through his gas tank and started the fire trail, as the car ended up hitting other parked cars in the lot. He had burn and inhalation injuries, as well as a cardiac arrest. Given the situation, one could determine I should have just called him deceased on the scene when we first found him unresponsive, we do have EMS protocols for traumatic issues. But I didn't, I wanted to save him.

I had a problem with the doctor's glance and the lack of confidence that the look put in me. Did he really view me as foolish with unrealistic expectations? I felt shame and disgraced that I didn't think the same way he did. I felt even worse when I told my partner and the engine crew the same thing. I was totally left second-guessing our actions. Did I waste time and skill on this patient? Did I do the right thing? Why didn't I look at the big picture and realize the situation myself?

> *"Guilt is just as powerful, but its influence is positive,*
> *while shame's is destructive. Shame erodes our courage*
> *and fuels disengagement."*
> — *Brene Brown PhD*

I got mad. I was angry the entire rest of the day and didn't say much to anyone. I just kept replaying the events in my head, going through the whole incident over and over. I kept replaying in my mind how the doctor looked at me. I'm supposed to be a professional. I'm supposed to know better and be better. Why did I try so hard?

After a few days of running this through my mind, I concluded that I did what I did because when I looked at the man, I saw my grandpa. I wanted to save him because he might be someone else's grandfather or dad. I wanted to do my best to bring him back to his family.

I felt angry at the doctor for having such a defeatist attitude. I shouldn't feel ashamed of what I did. He should. I was defensive. I was in denial. I didn't want to admit the doctor was right. I still think we did the right thing with our patient. I know the situation was bad and, looking back on it in hindsight, we should've thought differently—but in the end, we are in this profession to do all we can do.

We strive to beat death and to always win. We are often on the losing end of things. This makes our job difficult, and a person can brood on shame. It can lead to other issues, such as second-guessing yourself and failing to act quickly when necessary.

As a teacher, we need to share these types of experiences with our students and peers. We are not built to lose, but we need to understand we will lose, and we will lose often, especially in the game of life and medical emergencies. As I said before, we don't start the emergencies, but when we respond, all we can do is our best to resolve it. Sometimes we can, and sometimes we can't. In any case, feeling shameful for trying your best is not the answer.

Always do your best, no matter what. Treat the situation as if it were your family or friends. What would you want to be done? How hard would you try? What would you sacrifice? I tried my best to help, and it is hard to rationalize that the effort you make will not matter.

Part of life is knowing when to give up, as well. It's important to know when to say no. Sometimes it just is not meant to be. In the moment, we often do not see that. Monday morning quarterbacking, we may see things we overlooked or did not adjust to. Guilt can help us make changes to our future responses but having shame for trying your best is not the answer.

Use the guilt and frustration you feel to improve yourself and find new ways to look at situations. I admit I do that a lot more now. I try to take a broader view of the incident when I am walking up to it. I try to get a big picture and assign roles for the team. If you are the one in charge, then you need to lead. We have enough to deal with in this job, so try to help your students or team avoid second-guessing and shame.

Training About Death

In all the hundreds of hours of training I took for being a firefighter/paramedic, never was there any discussion about telling a family their loved one had died. The topic was never brought up or mentioned, but having been in emergency services for twenty years, I have had that discussion hundreds of times. It is never easy to do this. Telling someone their loved one is gone and not coming back is crushing. I dread having to do it.

As a preceptor and training officer for our department, I make sure the 'death talk' happens. I explain to the young probationary members the need to keep it short and to the point. Do not say things like "They have passed," because that can lead to questions like "Passed where?" or "Have gone where?" This is not the time to have large philosophical debates, nor do we all know what religious beliefs people have. Never assume.

I employ the method of saying, "I'm sorry for your loss. (Name of person) has died."

I'll leave it at that. If they have further questions, answer with generalities. Remember, you are not the medical examiner. You cannot say exactly what happened or how the person died. Often, I say we did our best. I change the topic to contacting relatives or friends. Often, with our calls, we have police officers on the scene who step in and take a lot of the notifications. They do a great job and must stay on the scene longer than we do.

When I did my death talk training, I found there was already a similar training aid out there. The acronym for use in training on how to deliver bad news is the pneumonic GRIEV_ING (11).

G- *Gather the family or other members present.*

R - *Seek out resources to help with grief, such as religious, family, and friends.*

I – *Identify yourself and name the deceased by name.*

E – *Educate the family or friends to the brief events and information that you do know.*

V – *Be clear and verify that the patient has died or is dead.*

(_) – *Space is just that, giving a moment to let the news set in.*

I – *Inquire or ask if there are any questions.*

N – *Nuts and bolts… offer the members to say goodbye to the body.*

G – *Give them contact information or resources to assist.*

A few years back, I was precepting a young member. We arrived at a home to find an elderly woman who had died in her sleep. She had been deceased for a while and obviously had been gone for at least a full day. There was no need for any paramedics. The neighbor had come over to check on her because the daughter had not heard from her mother in a few days.

Police officers were also on the scene with us. I was speaking to the officer, and we were getting basic information on the deceased woman when we heard the house phone ring and the young member behind us talking. As we turned around, we heard him say, "I need to inform you that your mom has died."

Both our mouths dropped as we realized he must be talking to the daughter. "Yep, she's dead," he said, and then hung up. We looked back at each other, and I said, "Who was that?"

"The daughter," he said. "She was pretty upset. I could hardly understand what she was saying with all her crying."

The police officer then used his cell phone to call the daughter back. "Well, our work here is done." I said and took the new member out of the home and walked back out to our ambulance. I asked him, "What was all that about?" He said I told him to just be honest. I smiled to myself and told him, "Yes, but you also need to have some compassion."

It was funny at the time. He was so blunt and brutally honest. He was right, I told him to be honest, but the frankness and the tone also come into play. Think about how your message will be received and what tone of voice you will use to relay it. In these types of situations, obviously, a gentle touch is needed with a lot of compassion.

Roleplay these types of scenes with your students. Put them through the process of giving the bad news to family members. Go through the best-case and worst-case scenarios. Bring in other agencies that they will be working with on these types of scenes. Students need to be prepared to have this conversation because it will happen all the time. They need to be comfortable enough to say what needs to be said. They should realize it never gets easy. Give them the tools to succeed and let them apply their knowledge. Set them up for success.

Crime Scenes

All death scenes are crime scenes, but this is never talked about in class much either. Because they are crime scenes, police or LEO (law enforcement officers) are called, and they remain on the scene.

In the fire or EMS service, we arrive and make sure the person is deceased, then we leave. If the person is young and the circumstances are questionable, then there will most likely be an autopsy. The scene becomes a criminal investigation for the police. I have been to several drug overdoses where young people, usually in their 20s, have died. Those scenes are considered crime scenes because the person who sells the drugs could be charged criminally. There have been many deaths from overdoses that have been linked back to a single dealer who was found guilty of lacing the drugs with other substances, increasing their potency. The police are the ones who do the investigating. They often ask for our names and what we did in the room. They want to know what we touched or moved. They will also ask if anything was out of place on our arrival or if we noticed anything strange.

"Accuracy is the twin brother of honesty; inaccuracy of dishonesty."
—*Nathaniel Hawthorne*

This is again another concept that is unfamiliar to students. They need to know their EMS patient care reports, or their fire reports could be part of a criminal investigation. We often tell our students that their reports could be used in court, but we fail to teach them why that is and in what aspects they could be called to testify. Lawyers will pick the reports apart looking for anything to use in the case. A misspelled word could be construed that you are an incompetent person and therefore being incompetent at your job. Maybe that is why the patient died.

Everything in the report is fair game and because of that, the reports are incredibly important.

In my first year as fire chief, we had a pedestrian versus vehicle accident. I went with the ambulance crew. Upon our arrival, we saw a man had been run over between two apartment buildings. He was still under the car, near the trunk. As we moved the man away from the vehicle, I heard the driver shout, "I only looked down at my phone for a second!" Then he said, "Where did he even come from?"

We did our best, we stabilized the patient enough to be transported, but he eventually died of his injuries. I made sure that the statements were put in our reports. The police used them to charge the man driving the vehicle. He denied he made the statements, but his cell phone records showed he was texting when he was driving the vehicle as it struck the man, going over the posted speed limit in a parking area.

Most classes don't focus on what to write in reports Take the time to teach your students how important it is to get things right in these types of scenes. They can and will be used in criminal cases. Prepare examples of reports to demonstrate your point. Show different report styles and illustrate what an excellent report should look like.

Bring in your local law enforcement officials. Have the officers talk about what they would like the responders to do. The students should be able to answer basic questions, or at the very least, be able to understand they will be questioned by the officers when they arrive on the scene. They need to help the officers with their reports as well. Discuss with your students the interaction that needs to take place between all parties involved. Bring it to the medical examiner's office or coroner's office. Have a question-and-answer session devoted to the question, "What do we do when our patient dies, or we find a dead victim?"

Remember, we are all in this together. A proper choreography of these principles will help ensure success in the field. As the instructor, you should always be on the lookout for new and more innovative ways to reach your students. I have more ideas than I have time for in class. Write them down and keep a list. Finding new ways to challenge your students learning is the mark of a great teacher!

Mr. Hill's Notes:

- Death will be part of this job.

- Start the hard conversation with your students now.

- Give your students the tools and resources needed.

- Learn to cope with death successfully.

- You are not alone. Ask for help when you need it.

- Find positive activities to help yourself cope.

- Practice training on death.

My daughters and I at the Pancake Breakfast at the firehouse 2017
(Photo courtesy of the author)

Chapter Ten

WHERE DO WE GO FROM HERE?

"Teaching is the one profession that creates all other professions."
—*Unknown*

As I finish this book, I look back and it reminds me of what this work has been for me: a reflective journey. We all need to take time away from our busy schedules and reflect on the day. Whether you do it over coffee in the morning or on your morning commute, take the time to reflect and think about today and yesterday.

I had a chief once say she had a conversation with herself every morning about what she planned to achieve that day and what she planned to do better than yesterday. At first, I thought the need to have a plan set out was funny, but she was right. Sometimes we need to have checklists in our own minds about what to get done. I find myself more productive if I have something written down to accomplish. The feeling that comes with crossing out a 'to-do' item is satisfying.

In football, our coach told the players to do the mirror test. The mirror test requires you to look into the mirror and see your reflection. Ask yourself if you are getting better or getting worse. Basically, you face yourself. Be honest about what your participation, drive, determination, and effort have been. Sometimes we all need to do this. It is a good way to reset and check ourselves.

> *"I believe there's an inner power that makes winners or*
> *losers. And the winners are the ones who really listen to*
> *the truth of their hearts."*
> *—Sylvester Stallone*

Just a few years back, after a tough cardiac arrest call, my crew from Station 3 sat down in the kitchen to complete our own AAR (after-action report) together. Unfortunately, the call ended with our patient not surviving. The call had some difficult issues from the start. Our patient was a younger person. She was only in her 20s, and her medical emergency happened in a public restaurant kitchen. There was an unknown time of her being unconscious and unresponsive. We had to deal with many upset coworkers and family members afterward. I was the lead paramedic on the call, and my partner and I rehashed the events with our engine crew, who also responded to assist us. We started off by mentioning one or two items that I could have changed, but in the end, we all realized I tend to step in and do too many things. The Marc needs to improve list went from two to ten quickly.

As the lead paramedic, my role was to supervise and lead the action of the call. I'm supposed to step back, oversee the scene, and direct my fellow co-workers in our CRM (crew resource management) 'pit crew' mentality. However, I was the first to get to the patient. I checked her to ensure she was not responsive. I was the one who dragged her out of the bathroom and into an area where we could work on her better. I set up the monitor, and I got the medications out of the bag. After the automatic pulse generator was attached, I stepped in and intubated the patient after my partner missed his first attempt, and ensured an end-tidal (ETCO2) wave was activated. I pushed some of the drugs and delivered one of the cardiac shocks as well. I was deep in the scene and in the care of the patient. I was not doing what I was supposed to be doing.

One thing led to another as I put myself deeper into the situation. My partner said, "You know what your problem is? You need to stop doing something and just stand there!" We all laughed because it was so true. I didn't need to do anything but supervise and be the one in charge. That was the role I was supposed to play. I failed miserably. After all the years of service in this field and after all the training, certifications, awards, and education degrees I have received over twenty years, I still find myself pushing in and wanting to take over far too much. I needed to let go and step back. You think I would've learned after all this time.

Am I a micromanager? Do I not trust others? Why must I feel I need to be in charge? To be honest, some of those questions will be answered with an honest yes. In this job, I find myself doing more if my partner is new or inexperienced. I tend to push in and get too involved if things don't happen quickly. I know this and I really try not to, but it depends on the situation, as well. This is one of my personal demons. I trust others, and I completely trust and respect the people I work with, but I will say it takes time. As a teacher, realize you may have this same situation and you need to just step back, just let go, and stand there.

Not surprisingly, it has been difficult for me as a teacher to just let go and leave the students to their own devices. While it is okay to say no, the reality is that it is incredibly difficult to stand by and watch someone fail. This is especially true when you have spent many hours trying your best to convince and motivate them. Coming to the realization that you cannot save them all is frustrating. Letting go is hard, perhaps the most difficult thing you need to do as a teacher.

We get into this line of work to not fail but to accomplish the impossible. We strive to do it daily. Sometimes we fail even with our best efforts, and that is a hard pill to swallow. We need to realize that our best intentions, the million dollars of technology we use, or the best professional training we achieve don't always matter. In the end, sometimes it is not up to us. Occasionally we need to stop doing something and just stand there.

> *"If opportunity doesn't knock, build the door."*
> *—Milton Berle*

I wanted to write this book to help those who are interested in teaching and instructing the next generations. This book has specific topics related to emergency services and their singular training and education needs. It also has many ideas about how to be a great teacher and instructor.

I am by no means a perfect teacher. I am a work in progress. Education is a process of applying knowledge and a journey that only ends in the grave. Every day, we get better at being ourselves, or we get a bit worse. Hopefully, in our last breath, we will have had far better days than bad ones. I wanted this book to be part of those better days. I hope you found this book informative and have been able to take some lessons from it for yourselves.

I would be most happy if you decided to get more involved in the process of education. Every organization, whether it is a business, a fire department, an agency, organization, or a school, needs great teachers. I cannot think of one entity on this planet that does not require the services of a great instructor. We all learn the ways of the business we work for. I hope after reading this we can all agree and share our stories with each other.

Service and Self

Choosing to be a teacher is a lot like choosing to be in the emergency services field. It is a calling and a service to do the work. Teachers work to help people in any way possible. We do not do it for massive monetary gains or to be able to retire on our own islands. We become firefighters, paramedics, EMTs, hazmat technicians, rescue technicians, law enforcement officers, and many other emergency roles because we want to give back to our community and we want to make our communities better than we found them.

Becoming an emergency services teacher is just another step in the process of giving back and helping in any way we can. We are called to help the next generations and our coworkers because we enjoy seeing that light shine in their eyes. We enjoy helping our departments grow and progress.

You may find yourself in a team meeting where the supervisor is looking for mentors or field trainers. You look around and no one else is raising their hand; they are all looking at the floor, pretending no one sees them. You feel the need to do more. You look up and you raise your hand. Welcome to the party! You have just been selected to become the next teacher of the incoming probie class. Have no fear, you will make it—and you will be better for it. Your organization will appreciate you for all your hard work and effort.

Our students are our constituents. They are the ones we put in all the labor for. They are the ones we want to get to the next level. Our students are the reason we have a class to teach in the first place. Without them, we are nothing, and without us, they will not be able to achieve their goals. In this mutually beneficial relationship, we find many avenues to explore and stories to share. The students benefit from our instruction and from our experience. We benefit from reinforcing the subject material and from the feeling of satisfaction we have in seeing positive results. The community we serve is a special one that we were once a part of and now oversee. Let's make our constituents proud and make our community better.

Know your audience. Understand where they are coming from and what type of learners they are. Our students all come from many diverse backgrounds and social classes. To achieve and succeed as a teacher requires a true understanding of these many parts and how they all interact with one another. The income levels (SES), the family structures, past and current employment, life experiences, and generational changes over time all contribute to a wide and varied audience.

We all learn differently, and we all learn at our own pace. It is up to us to create a successful battle plan to achieve positive and progressive results at the end of the course. It is up to the teacher to define the goals and formulate the lessons that will raise all the achievement expectations to the stars.

"Start by doing what's necessary, then do what's possible;
and suddenly you are doing the impossible."
Francis of Assissi

Being a teacher is not about knowing it all. No one is perfect and no one can know everything. There are no true experts. All we can do is try our best. Being a teacher and a leader in learning is not about being an expert in the subjects that we teach. I used to teach Social Studies in public schools. How am I supposed to remember every person, event, time, cause, and crisis that has happened in the thousands of years of human history?

Teaching is about understanding how to best relay information to a diverse group of students and work with those students effectively and efficiently from start to finish. Great teachers rely on Gardner's levels of intelligence, Maslow's needs, and Bloom's Taxonomy. Education is about the process of growing your knowledge base and adapting to new information. You should have multiple activities in your courses and offer different learning projects. Varying the instruction will keep your class fun and interesting. Remember to use your students to help you where and when you can. Your job as a teacher is to spark the enlightenment within each student so it will burn brightly and continue to expand, growing their knowledge to true wisdom.

Having compassion and integrity will take you far in this profession. Putting your heart on the line and feeling for your students will make you a great teacher. However, we need to be careful with that trust and understanding. We must maintain standards and we must keep the rules of the organization sound. A great teacher will take all the challenges of teaching, as well as the students, into consideration when planning the lesson. The integrity a teacher must show is paramount to having a successful class. Being honest, open, and caring are only parts of what makes a teacher successful.

You can never over-communicate. Every deadly incident in the emergency services in some way goes back to communication. As teachers, it is up to us to be clear and concise in our words. We must acknowledge the communication cycle and understand how the system works. We must be listeners as well as speakers. We need to feel the room and understand that most communication in the classroom is non-verbal. Our communication must be clear so there are no gray areas where misunderstanding occurs. If we fail in this, then our students will fail.

Failure is not an option and can never be accepted. We cannot fail them. We must endeavor to champion the greatest speakers in the world and offer our best efforts to disseminate our subject material to our students, our constituents, and our community.

Believe in yourself and have a positive attitude. Take a breath and refocus your efforts when you feel your enthusiasm wane. Do not get down or have a poor attitude. Some days are more challenging than others, and sometimes your best intentions grow sour. Keep your chin up and keep pushing on. Learn from your mistakes. Evaluate what has worked for you and what has not. The only way we will ever get better at anything in life is if we learn from our mistakes.

Embrace your Mistakes and have Fun

Recently, I visited NASA's Kennedy Space Center, which has a fantastic array of information on the history of our journey to space, the moon, and beyond.

One exhibit shares the sad story of Apollo 1. The crew of three brave astronauts all died during a training accident. The first lunar capsules had 100% oxygen in them, which, as we know in this profession, is highly flammable. It only took a crossed circuit to start a small flame that spread throughout the capsule. But that wasn't the only problem. The first Apollo capsules had doors that were only able to be opened and locked from the outside. There was no emergency release or any way for the astronauts inside to get out. Once the spark ignited the oxygen it was over in a matter of seconds. After the tragedy, NASA put the entire lunar program on a year-long hiatus to evaluate and learn from the incident. They did their own AARs.

Everyone makes mistakes. I've tried to share what has worked for me and do my best to illustrate those views. However, my way is not the only one. Adapt to your own needs and find your path. Make it your own.

Be engaging and a storyteller. Getting to this point in the book means you have read plenty of my stories. Stories tell tales. They are awesome tools to set the mood and to teach lessons. Students will remember the stories you tell, and they will pass them along.

Sometimes the stories you tell can be fun. My students especially loved my ghost stories and the strange lights in the night sky. All my stories are true tales as well. I would hold those special stories until the end of class or for special occasions. I would even use them as rewards if the students were able to achieve high grades. The students wanted a story more than candy!

Make learning enjoyable. Be the teacher you wish you had. Be an example others will want to emulate. It is a great feeling when you run into your past students and see the delight on their faces. It's wonderful to hear how much they enjoyed having you as their teacher. It is a thorough joy. It is what makes this job worth it. Knowing you have a positive effect on your students gets you through a lot of the rough days.

Make this job one that you enjoy, and do not make it into a prison sentence. Include competition for fun. People in this field love competition. They thrive on it. If you make activities or lessons into a game or pit parts of the class against each other, you will be amazed by the results.

"Accept the things to which fate binds you, and love the people with whom fate brings you together, but do so with all your heart."
—*Marcus Aurelius*

When I was chief, I had a large group of new firefighters that I needed to train as soon as possible. After the third day, I thought, "How am I going to get all of this done in the next two weeks?" I mentioned it to one of the officers who was helping me with the training, and he said, "Let's pit one group against another and see who finishes first."

We put the class into three groups and gave them a list of the objectives and needed training items. The students taught themselves! We supervised everything they did, and they needed to check in with us to approve of their skills, but they did it. It was a major motivating factor for them. They wanted to get it done first and best. Not only did I approve of the skill checks, but I also gave them a certain number of stars as a grade, with four stars being the best. It was a competition to see who could get the most stars in the shortest time. It was fun, and they enjoyed themselves. It also built team spirit, and the other members of the department wanted to do it as well. Remember, you have the power to make it as easy and as rewarding as you want, but you can also make it difficult and laborious too.

There are many ways to train, but the best ways use real-world examples and situations. Whether it is role-playing or talking and walking through how to accomplish a task like catching a hydrant, use real-life examples. Make learning interesting by creating situations where the student uses higher learning skills and make their brains coordinate several tasks. Use multiple departments or services as they would be. Utilize the tools you work with and do not waste time training with tools you will never use again. Train as if their lives depend on it because in this career, they do. The little things add up. Strive for perfection but settle for greatness.

This is a stressful career. I thought I knew this, but I had no idea until I did it full-time. Teaching was stressful, and I was sometimes exhausted from thinking so much. Being a firefighter or paramedic brings a different kind of exhaustion. Sometimes I felt like I got run over by a bus and then backed over by a dump truck.

Being in the emergency services is filled with both micro and macro-stresses. A large part of training and education should be focused on stressors. Find ways to deal with them and help your students find positive ways to cope. Help them by talking about death and about the stresses that they will have in this career. Educate them about the many ways people cope in a positive and productive manner. It is imperative they understand they are never alone.

As teachers, it is up to us to create a positive classroom environment where everyone can share and feel safe. Your students need to know death will be a major part of this job, and it will never get easy. They will go to the funerals of retirees and coworkers who have passed away. How they deal with this and how their departments cope with this will all have a major effect on their lives. I beg you to find ways to teach them in a manner that will allow them to thrive, rather than becoming another suicide statistic.

Finally, I implore you to learn from my mistakes and find your own path. I can only offer what I have seen and dealt with in my life. These are my stories and my experiences. Think about what I have worked to accomplish with this book. I hope you have enjoyed the stories, that you learned something new, and that you will take the next steps toward being a better you.

Until we meet again… stay safe out there.

Mr. Hill's Notes:

- Always try your best no matter what.

- Sometimes you need to step back and take a breath.

- You will fail sometimes. Pick yourself up, learn, and move on.

- Positive attitudes are contagious.

- You don't need to know it all.

- Be the teacher you would want to have.

- Have fun and enjoy the journey.

Vertical ventilation (roof) training 2018. Teaching new techniques and skills. (Photo courtesy of author)

Afterword

Writing this book has taken me years to accomplish. I started to write this book when I was off duty with my second back injury and ended up finishing the book when I was off duty with my third back injury. (The bottom line is to make sure you take care of yourself and call for lifting assistance!)

What I have learned throughout the process of writing this book is that even though there are many books on education, learning, and on many of the subjects I talked about, no one has said it the way I can. My voice is unique and the experiences I have had over the years have taught me many great lessons.

Even though there are many opinions in the world, yours is special, and you should take the time to share what you have learned with others. Anytime you can give of yourself, you are doing a good thing. It doesn't have to be big either. Just being there to listen is the simplest, but sometimes best, act a person can do.

I hope you found value in this book. My intention has always been to create a resource guide for those who have found themselves teaching something that they may have never been formally taught.

"No act of kindness, no matter how small, is ever wasted."
—Aesop

Being an educator is a special calling and one in which I have found significant value. It is something that I fell into, but it's something I love doing.

The world needs more educators. I hope you will take this resource and share it with others who think may find value in it. Remember, you can always find help and assistance when in need. You just have to ask!

Visit the official webpage at www.twodarkthirty.com

Works Cited

1. Psychology Today Staff. Psychology Today. *Imposter Syndrome*. [Online] 2022. https://www.psychologytoday.com/us/basics/imposter-syndrome.

2. Kurt, Dr. Serhat. Maslow's Hierarchy of Needs in Education. *Educational Psychology*. [Online] February 6, 2020. https://educationlibrary.org/maslows-hierarchy-of-needs-in-education/.

3. Various assistants, Instructional guide for university faculty and teaching. Howard Gardner's Theory of Multiple Intelligences. *Northern Illinois University Center for Innovative Teaching and Learning*. [Online] 2020. https://www.niu.edu/citl/resources/guides/instructional-guide/gardners-theory-of-multiple-intelligences.shtml.

4. Unknown. Ways to Use Bloom's Taxonomy in Teaching. *Emporia State University.* [Online] March 3, 2021. https://online.emporia.edu/articles/education/use-blooms-taxonomy.aspx.

5. Devol, Philip E. *Getting Ahead in a Just-Gettin'-By World.* Highlands, TX : Aha! Process, Inc., April 12, 2004.

6. Unknown. Generational Differences in the Workplace. *Purdue University Global.* [Online] 2022. https://www.purdueglobal.edu/education-partnerships/generational-workforce-differences-infographic/.

7. Fry, Kristen Bialik and Richard. Millennial life: How young adulthood today compares with prior generations. *Pew Research.* [Online] February 14, 2019. https://www.pewresearch.org/social-trends/2019/02/14/millennial-life-how-young-adulthood-today-compares-with-prior-generations-2/

8. Duignan, Brian. Dunning-Kruger effect. *Britanica.com.* [Online] Encyclopedia Britannica, September 8, 2020. [Cited: June 3, 2022.] https://www.britannica.com/science/Dunning-Kruger-effect.

9. Graham, Gordon. High-Risk, Low-Frequency Events in Public Safety. *Lexipol.* [Online] July 15, 2020. https://www.lexipol.com/resources/blog/high-risk-lo

w-frequency-events-in-public-safety/.

10. Muriel A. Hagenaars, Emily A. Holmes, Fayette Klaassen, and Bernet Elzinga. Tetris and Word games lead to fewer intrusive memories when applied several days after analogue trauma. *National Library of Medicine.* [Online] October 31, 2017. https://www.ncbi.nlm.nih.gov/pmc/articles/PMC5678449/.

11. *Death in the field: Teaching paramedics to deliver effective death notifications using the educational intervention 'GRIEV_ING.'*. Hobgood C, Mathew D, Woodyard DJ, et al. 2013: 17 (4), Prehosp Emerg Care, pp. 201-510.

INDEX

Made in the USA
Las Vegas, NV
25 November 2023